Thank you...

... to the professionals, who were excited about our work, applauded our efforts, and encouraged us to pass it on.

... to the educators, who recognized the need and the responsibility, and readily reached out for help when death touched their school.

... to the young people, who shared their fears, their pain and their healing.

DEATH AND THE CLASSROOM

A Teacher's Guide to Assist Grieving Students

Kathleen Kidder Cassini and Jacqueline L. Rogers

Griefwork of Cincinnati, Inc., 1445 Colonial Drive, Suite B
Cincinnati, Ohio 45238

GRIEFWORK OF CINCINNATI, INC.
1445 Colonial Drive, Suite B
Cincinnati, Ohio 45238

Library of Congress Catalog Card Number 89-85498

ISBN #0-9627002-1-5

Layout and Cover Design: Alan Kastner

Foreword

Death and the Classroom is a teacher's ideal textbook for situations in which a teacher comes face-to-face with death in the school setting and must face his/her pupils' questions, feelings and fears. It is a down-to-earth presentation of the "how-to's" (a teacher's delight), with suggestions that are powerful, but easy to follow. But, it is much more than that.

Kahlil Gibran, in his book *The Prophet,* speaks of teachers:

> *"If he is indeed wise, he does not bid you*
> *enter the house of his wisdom,*
> *but rather leads you to the threshold*
> *of your own mind."*

Cassini and Rogers have exemplified this advice in their textbook... they will lead you to the threshold of your own mind regarding the psychology of death and, with their examples and suggestions will wisely guide you in developing your own repertoire of skills in teaching your pupils one of life's most important lessons.

Christa McAuliffe, the teacher/astronaut who died so tragically in the explosion of the Challenger, left a beautiful legacy to all teachers when she said: *"I touch the future... I teach."* What more beautiful and rewarding a charge could a teacher have than to touch the future lives of each of his/her students with regard to the development of a realistic and wholesome outlook toward the life cycle? In fact, a teacher's contribution in this area may well be the most important lesson a pupil learns - one that will be with him/her far longer than the facts of history or the experiments in science.

To touch death and be touched by death is profound, and is a part of the life and death cycle experience of every living person. Teachers are integral to this cycle for their task is to prepare their charges to live this cycle holistically: intellectually, spiritually, psychologically and physically; to "lead them to the threshold of their own minds." Until now, the psychological and spiritual aspects of death have been poorly addressed or not at all. This landmark text will serve as an important resource for teachers to address that void and fulfill that teaching mandate.

Jacqueline Kowalski, S.C. Ed.D.

Contents

Preface

Grieving people of all ages require support, patience and time as they tackle their griefwork.

The admirable qualities that make you a good educator may be just what creates your stumbling block when dealing with the grieving. If you are successful in your profession you are most likely the personality type that prefers to be organized and prepared for any situation.

We will also assume that you present a topic only after you have researched and outlined the subject matter and have a firm mental grasp of the material contained in your lesson plan. You are probably most comfortable when "all your ducks are in a row."

In an environment where "...the becoming is everything," where one is always working towards tomorrow, or next year, where everyone from the principal to the first grader is goal oriented, death is rarely part of the agenda.

When the school community experiences a death, it is like someone has dropped a monkey wrench into the machinery and everything comes to a standstill. One quickly finds that getting on with the business of the day is difficult at best.

Teachers are constantly asked to assume more responsibilities. When a death occurs, the need to deal with that loss cannot be avoided. One either responds well or poorly. What we propose in no way takes the place of the grieving student's parents, friends, relatives, clergy person, or community. We are asking you to recognize that you are part of that support system. You are in a position to augment and complement what others are already offering the student. In your day to day exposure to the student you will observe and react to grief related behavior.

In the last decade, thanks to talk shows, survivor support group efforts and newsprint articles, we have all been made aware that a death is not "handled" or "managed." Griefwork is always an individualized task.

As you observe the grieving, some common threads will become apparent. You will always see pain and confusion. You will recognize the student's inability to concentrate on the task at hand. Inadvertently forcing students to shelve their feelings of loss, anger, confusion and pain will create missed opportunities that cannot be recaptured.

When a student is ridiculed or ignored because of his inability to maintain his previous level of grades, attention span, or emotional stability, he will be forced to hide his grief, act out his anger and fears, or just quit school.

Your student will not just "get over" the death of someone who was an integral part of his/her world. We ask that you not set a time frame and expect him/her to meet your expectations.

We will introduce some guidelines that evolved from our listening to grieving people who have reached a level of acceptance. This compilation of suggestions in no way infers that our way is the only way to support grieving students in your classroom, but we do know our prescribed manner has been accepted and appreciated by those we have worked with over the past thirteen years.

We acknowledge that it will be difficult to remain objective when you are faced with not only the needs of your students, but your own vulnerability. We have all cultivated individual responses to death through our cultural and environmental backgrounds. Many misconceptions about how to assist the grieving have been with each of us since childhood. We have written *Death and the Classroom* with the hope that you and your students will profit by our experience and observations.

K.K.C. and J.L.R.

See This Child

See this child before you
   wounded
   vulnerable
   changed
   … the child of yesterday gone forever.
Who will really look at this child?
   Is it easier to assume
   he will emerge unscathed
   than to face the turmoil with him?
Who will step into the road
   before this child…
   laden with mountains and valleys,
   potholes and detours?
Who will walk a bit of his journey with him?
Who will offer some temporary shelter
   from the storms that rage around
   and within this child?
Who will open doors that this child
   cannot see through his pain?
Who will listen to what this child
   is really saying
   when he is belligerent
   when he is too shy to speak
   when his laughter masks his fears?
Who will help this child to recognize
   his successes,
   and give him the courage to step
   beyond his failures with dignity?
Who will be with this child
   on the other side of healing
   as he recognizes his growth
   and acceptance?

TEACHER AWARENESS

We could not resist giving you a quiz:

NORMAL/ABNORMAL GRIEF REACTIONS QUIZ

Following are some general observations noted by teachers of grieving students. Use the scenario that the father of a student in your classroom was killed suddenly in an industrial accident at the beginning of the school year. Please note if, over the remainder of the school year, you would find each of the following behaviors to be NORMAL (N) OR ABNORMAL (A):

1. (   )   Student retells events of father's death and funeral.
2. (   )   Student dwells on all the things he used to do with his/her father.
3. (   )   Student is disruptive in class.
4. (   )   Student uses excuse s/he cannot concentrate when s/he fails to complete school work.
5. (   )   Student instigates fights.
6. (   )   Student rejects old friend and teams up with classmate whose parent is also dead.
7   (   )   Student has become the "Class Clown".
8. (   )   Student is pre-occupied with medical causes of father's death.
9. (   )   Student spends free time walking or sitting alone.
10. (   )   Student, at times, appears unmoved by death of father.
11. (   )   Student seems overly sensitive or tearful.
12. (   )   Student drops out of afterschool activities.
13. (   )   Student assumes role of dead parent.
14. (   )   Student mentions talking to dead parent.
15. (   )   Student relates dreams about father.
16. (   )   Student attempts to call home often during school hours.
17. (   )   Student is pre-occupied with his/her own health.

STRESSFUL/COMFORTING COMMENTS QUIZ

Please read the following comments. Mark whether your grieving student, Bernard, would find your words COMFORTING (C) or STRESSFUL (S).

1. (   )   "Your father was a good man, Bernard. God loved your father so much he took him to Heaven."
2. (   )   "Be strong for your mother, and your brothers and sisters."
3. (   )   "The ways of God are a mystery. It was God's will."
4. (   )   "I know just how you feel, Bernard."
5. (   )   "Trust God, Bernard. He always has a good reason for what He does."
6. (   )   "It was for the best that your father didn't live. He is better off not suffering."
7. (   )   "It could be worse, Bernard. Remember, you still have your mother."
8. (   )   "I could never handle this as well as you."
9. (   )   "You just need a little time."
10. (   )   "Your father would want you to be brave."

QUIZ RESULTS: NORMAL/ABNORMAL GRIEF REACTIONS

If you completed this quiz, you may have found that all the behavioral responses could be NORMAL.

1. STUDENT RETELLS EVENTS OF FATHER'S DEATH AND FUNERAL.
    Retelling the event of a parent's death over and over is the young person's way of internalizing, reliving the event to convince him/herself of its reality. S/he simply needs an acknowledgment of the story, and of how hard this event is to tolerate.

2. STUDENT DWELLS ON ALL THE THINGS S/HE USED TO DO WITH HIS/HER FATHER.
    When the dreams and plans for the future are crushed, it is only natural to cling to the past. How comforting to recall all the good times, the fun times and the safe times with the parent who died! The student needs to recall these times so s/he can say his/her goodbyes. The student is also saying goodbye to dreams of events which could have been shared with that parent in the future.

3. STUDENT IS DISRUPTIVE IN CLASS
    The teacher does not have to tolerate disruptive behavior in the classroom. The student is scared and is reaching out for help. Contact the school counselor, psychologist, or a bereavement specialist.

4. STUDENT USES EXCUSE S/HE CANNOT CONCENTRATE AND FAILS TO COMPLETE SCHOOL WORK.

    The student is telling the truth. Priorities have been severely altered. The grieving student will find it very difficult to concentrate. Grieving people do not choose when to feel confused or out of control.

    The astute teacher may find s/he is able to excuse the student from some paperwork, with the understanding that the student will be responsible for knowing core material.

5. STUDENT INSTIGATES FIGHTS.

    The teacher will often notice that the grieving student is defiant, insolent, or intolerant. When a grieving student is involved in an altercation, s/he must pay the consequences for his/her actions; at the same time, the source of his/her anger must be investigated. The source of this anger can be traced to the death of his/her father, and this is a normal response.

6. STUDENT REJECTS OLD FRIENDS AND TEAMS UP WITH CLASSMATE WHOSE PARENT IS ALSO DEAD.

    Grieving people seek out others who can relate to their pain. Students who have experienced loss through death unwillingly and tragically belong to an exclusive club. In the company of each other, they probably feel comfortable.

7. STUDENT HAS BECOME "CLASS CLOWN."

    Young people worry about how others view them. Do they fit in with their peers, or are they different? The death of a parent or sibling may label a student as "different". When the young person's self-esteem is low, he may use inappropriate behavior to gain the extra attention he needs at this time. Redirect his negative energies toward a class project or activity where he can excel and keep his behavior in your classroom from becoming disruptive.

8. YOU FIND OUT THAT STUDENT IS PRE-OCCUPIED WITH MEDICAL CIRCUMSTANCES OF DEATH.

    The grieving student simply may not have been included when the medical information was given, so s/he is curious and has a right to have questions answered. Without being given the facts about an accident, the young person may wonder if his father's legs were crushed, or his back was burned, or did the hospital have to hook him to a machine so he could breathe. When death is the result of a disease, family members may experience anxiety regarding the possibility that they, too, may catch or develop the same disease. This anxiety can be relieved by undergoing a medical examination with the family physician. Even a young child needs to be assured that he is healthy. The surviving parent should be notified of the student's concern and anxiety.

9. STUDENT SPENDS RECESS TIME WALKING OR SITTING ALONE.

If the student is no longer synchronized with the world around him/her, s/he perceives himself/herself as being alone. Is this student alone by choice, or has s/he been ostracized by peers? If the student is alone by choice, s/he may need this time to re-group and sort through feelings. If the student has been ostracized by peers, the teacher needs to ascertain what is precipitating this behavior.

10. AT TIMES, STUDENT APPEARS UNMOVED BY DEATH OF PARENT.

The key words are "at times". When the young person has experienced enough painful thoughts or memories for that hour, as a protective mechanism s/he may close the door to that part of the mind and simply go outside and ride a bike, shoot some baskets or take a walk.

11. STUDENT SEEMS OVERLY-SENSITIVE OR TEARFUL.

Grieving hurts. How can a young person be overly-sensitive to the death of a family member? If becoming overwhelmed makes the grieving student uncomfortable when s/he is in the classroom setting, silently excuse him/her to go to a pre-arranged safe place.

12. STUDENT DROPS OUT OF AFTERSCHOOL ACTIVITIES.

The student simply may not have the time or energy to continue afterschool activities, or may feel guilty enjoying them. Give the student the opportunity to explain reasons for dropping the activity, offer options, but then abide by his/her decisions. The student may only need reassurance that it would be a healthy decision to continue with afterschool activities.

13. STUDENT ASSUMES THE ROLE OF DEAD PARENT.

Often the grieving young person will assume the tasks or the personality of the parent who died, in an attempt to fill the great void in the family structure. The family must work through this period of adjustment. The student should in no way be given the idea that s/he is expected to take the place of the parent who died.

14. STUDENT MENTIONS TALKING TO DEAD PARENT.

After relying on, trusting in, counting on, or bouncing off the same person his/her entire life, it is not uncommon to continue that habit when confused or distressed. It is normal for the student to be in no hurry to give up the relationship once shared with the dead parent.

15. STUDENT RELATES DREAMS ABOUT FATHER.

Our dreams reflect the subjects our waking thoughts have not finished digesting. These dreams are not necessarily nightmares. Letting go is a lengthy process.

16. STUDENT ATTEMPTS TO CALL HOME OFTEN DURING SCHOOL HOURS.

We can never anticipate the anxiety of a grieving young person when separated from the surviving parent. Arrange appropriate times during the school day when the student can call home. This activity should be permitted but given structure… "You may call during library, lunch, and study hall." The student needs to be assured that the surviving parent is still alive.

17. STUDENT IS PRE-OCCUPIED WITH HIS OWN HEALTH.

The reality of the death has made the student conscious of his/her own mortality. The young person can experience anxiety regarding the possibility that s/he, too, could be killed. When a sibling or parent dies of disease, the student may worry that s/he, too, could catch or develop whatever disease killed his/her family member. A sensitive family doctor can perform a routine physical examination and assuage the fear by verifying the good health of the young person. It is important that the teacher not minimize the student's concern. The surviving parent or adult sibling should be notified.

QUIZ RESULTS: STRESSFUL/COMFORTING COMMENTS

If you have completed this quiz, you may have found that all the comments made could be STRESSFUL.

1. "YOUR FATHER WAS A GOOD MAN, BERNARD. GOD LOVED YOUR FATHER SO MUCH HE TOOK HIM TO HEAVEN."

A young person's immature concept of God is easily distorted. S/he may decide to refrain from being good, fearing s/he could also be called to Heaven.

2. "BE STRONG FOR YOUR MOTHER, AND YOUR BROTHERS AND SIS-TERS."

No student should ever be made to think s/he must assume the role of the dead parent. A young person cannot sacrifice feelings or disguise emotions for the sake of other grieving family members.

3. "THE WAYS OF GOD ARE A MYSTERY. IT WAS GOD'S WILL."

God is a creator of life, not a taker of life. Our bodies succumb to illness, disease, accident or outside forces.

4. "I KNOW JUST HOW YOU FEEL, BERNARD."

The grief of each student is unique, even though the circumstances of death may appear similar. Many young people have a hard enough time expressing themselves;

suggesting that our feelings and responses are identical only closes the door to the grieving student verbalizing his/her fear and pain. No one can know how another individual feels, we can only imagine. It may be well-chosen to say "I don't know what you are feeling, but I care about your pain. If you would like to talk, I will listen."

5. "TRUST GOD, BERNARD. HE ALWAYS HAS A GOOD REASON FOR WHAT HE DOES."

The young person needs to be assured that God does not cause death to teach us a lesson, and a young person will find no plausible reason good enough to explain a parent's death.

6. "IT WAS FOR THE BEST THAT YOUR FATHER DIDN'T LIVE. HE IS BETTER OFF NOT SUFFERING."

A student may prefer to have a suffering father: a father to touch, talk with, ask questions of, than no father at all.

7. "IT COULD BE WORSE, BERNARD. YOU STILL HAVE YOUR MOTHER."

What the young person hears is "Watch out, your mother could be next!" How could your student find comfort in contemplating the thought of losing his mother as well? When one is suffering and hurting, statements like the above are the proverbial slap on the back..."Look at the bright side...shape up...others are worse off than you...!"

8. "I COULD NEVER HANDLE THIS AS WELL AS YOU."

Putting the grieving student on a pedestal leaves him nowhere to turn after the inevitable fall. The grieving student needs to respond: "If you see me as handling this death, you are distorting the picture. I am barely holding on."

9. "YOU JUST NEED A LITTLE TIME."

Time does not heal, it is what a person does with the time that is important. Grieving is hard work. It is insulting to minimize what the grieving student is facing. That "little time" involves years of yearning, missing, wishing, and wondering what life would have been like with a father included.

10. "YOUR FATHER WOULD WANT YOU TO BE BRAVE."

Bravery is a cumbersome burden to carry when one's heart is breaking. A son or daughter needs to hear, "Your father loved you, and would not wish you to be brave. Your father would want caring adults to remain available to you and comfort you. He would want you to identify and acknowledge your feelings, so you might work through your grief and, eventually, arrive at a place of acceptance."

II

AGE LEVELS - A STUDENT'S CONCEPTION OF DEATH

Teachers are aware that children of the same chronological age will display a wide variety of intellectual and emotional responses to any given situation.

In the following paragraphs we will discuss the maturing of a child's view of death. As the teacher, your responsibility will be to discover where each student fits into the maturation process, regardless of chronological age.

Children of all ages need to grieve and mourn the death of a significant person. They need to know the truth. They need to work through the separation. They must be permitted to verbalize their feelings.

Before the age of three (or the age of language) the child lacks the ability for conceptual thought but does experience separation and loss.

At the time of his four-year-old sister's death following a long illness, a two-and-one-half-year-old boy asked his father, " Do little boys die too? "

Children, ages three and four, think of death as being temporary: a temporary sleep. They do not grasp the concept of final limits. There is only NOW. Life is simply a matter of being asleep and being awake. Although these children have an impressive command of language, be cautious of the words you use. Refrain from telling children that Grandma went to sleep and is in heaven. Using the word "sleep" in your explanation will confuse the child and may result in the child being fearful of going to bed. Refrain from using the word "lost" when announcing a death... "We lost dear Aunt Ellie last Tuesday." The child may translate this statement literally.

It is better to explain that when people are very old or very, very sick, sometimes they die. Keep in mind that to the small child, all adults are old. Yes, everyone eventually dies.

The child needs to be told that "...when a person is dead, he no longer feels the cold or the heat. She does not feel pain. His heart does not beat. Her lungs do not take in air."

By the age of three, most children have an impressive command of language. Curiosity is a strong trait and, as a result, when the child thinks about the topic of death s/he will share his/her thoughts with adults.

Nicholas, age four, had asked many questions about the death of his grandmother and was obviously comfortable speaking of it to adults. He entered the funeral home viewing room where his grandmother's body was laid out in the large wood casket. His grandmother's head was nestled in a pillow covered with the same material used to upholster the slanted open casket lid. The bottom half of the wood casket lid was closed, concealing the lower portion of her body. All Nicholas saw was grandmother's head, chest and arms surrounded by upholstery material and wood. He studied the scene before him and a look of concern came over his face as he asked, "Why did they make Granny into a couch?"

An adult helped Nicholas define the parts of the casket and showed the child Granny's feet and legs. A large problem had a simple solution.

When an adult lies and a child is told that "Auntie went on a long trip and is not coming back...", the child can feel deserted. Some adults mistakenly feel that a half truth will upset a child less than the facts. Children will find no comfort in being shielded from the truth. If the adult will not talk about death with him/her, the child will continue to think about death but on his/her own terms, utilizing a vivid imagination.

To the young child, death is reversible. If it happens, it can "un-happen." To the three-and-four-year-old, there is no final or forever. They may ask repeatedly when Grandpa is going to stop being dead and come back and play with them.

One young newly widowed mother was initially distressed when her preschool children played house. They would declare an identity to begin the play: "I'm the mommy and you are the daddy so lay down and be dead." Later in the game Daddy would be alive.

Children of this age cannot distinguish between the animate and the inanimate. They perceive the dead person as being able to walk, talk, and eat. They will ask if Daddy is hungry in heaven or ask if Grandma still goes fishing.

In the world of the young child, everything is associated: "Grandmother went to the hospital. Grandmother died." The conclusion is that when someone goes to the hospital - they die.

We must be very clear when talking with a child about death. "Yes, Grandmother died in the hospital. She died because she was very sick. Her heart was very old and could not be fixed. Most people who go to the hospital are given medicine or have an operation, and they return to their homes to do all the things they used to do."

By the age of five most children become aware that death is something significant and disruptive and that one becomes "all dead". They begin to realize that death is permanent. They perceive death as a person, a skeleton, a creature in the night, or a ghost. Death is scary.

They see death as an accident, a special happening in a special situation. "If you get runned over, then you are dead." A five year old's vocabulary can include such words as coffin, cemetery, cancer. The child will tend to imagine things more frightening than the actual facts concerning the death. The child needs explanations and reassurance.

A few years ago the actor who played Mr. Hooper on the Sesame Street children's television show died. The writers of the show responsibly decided to discuss the death on the air. The young viewers watched the residents of Sesame Street talk with a child on the show and acknowledge the death. They simply and honestly explained to the child that Mr. Hooper could never come back again. The child asked questions that centered on his own needs. These natural concerns were answered by the adults. The child needed to be told there were other adults who might read to him or fix him milk shakes now that Mr. Hooper was dead. The adults agreed Sesame Street would miss Mr. Hooper, and things would never be the same. The adults reminded the child that they had shared memories, were lucky to have known Mr. Hooper and everyone on Sesame Street could look forward to eventually being happy once again.

By the age of six the child begins to understand death as absolute, final, comprehensive, and personal. They may fear that someone they know will die. They tend to talk less about death than they did at ages three to five. They usually equate death with old age and consider childhood death unnatural.

The six-year-old may react to death with anger or hostility. "I hate Mommy for dying." It is important to show the child that you understand he/she is hurting.

Ages seven, eight, and nine usually have many questions. These questions are asked out of natural curiosity. This age group is intrigued with the workings of the body and its functions. After you present the facts concerning a specific death, we suggest you handle the topic of death education as you would sex education. Be truthful and only offer as much information as is needed to satisfy the questions raised.

A student may ask, "How do they know when a person is really dead?" The teacher can simply explain how the body's vital signs are recorded by a physician before the person can be pronounced dead. The seven, eight, or nine-year-old may ask about decomposition or continued growth of teeth and fingernails. These questions from the child are sincere and not meant to be macabre.

For a week or so after the death the child in this age group may still entertain the fantasy that the dead person will return. They usually understand the separation of body and spirit.

You may perceive the child as going on as if nothing has happened. S/he may appear to daydream and retreat into his/her own world, or may listen to you for a time and then change the subject. If you are patient the child will return later to continue the discussion.

Often adults are shocked because they perceive the child as being selfish. "He died and he promised to take me to Disneyland." "She died, so now who will take me to the beach?" The child's world has enlarged, but the child's focus is still on "self".

By the age of ten, the child usually sees death as the final and unavoidable conclusion to life. The young person clearly knows the difference between alive and dead, and understands feelings of loss, both his/her own and the feelings of others. S/he becomes concerned for the other survivors of the death and worries about their well being and future. S/he may need to verbalize concern about the loneliness of a newly widowed parent or grandparent.

By the time a child enters adolescence, s/he has developed a pattern of coping skills which seem to work for him/her. Depending on these learned responses, the adolescent enters this difficult period of development more (or less) equipped to survive a trauma successfully. Living in a state of flux is normal for the adolescent, in addition to the fact that coping mechanisms are different for each individual. It is essential that the adults in his/her world be prepared to accept his/her vacillating needs as expected and normal.

Adolescents will eventually intellectualize on the topic of death. This often includes investigating their religious and philosophical views about life after death. Although they may appear pre-occupied with death, they do not believe it will ever happen to them. They are future oriented. They have plans to make and things to do. Death is an enemy.

Adolescents may appear unstable. They will ask questions and then act as if they don't want your answers. Emotions are in the forefront with adolescents in any discussion of death.

A junior high school teacher did not anticipate the reaction she experienced when she announced to her class that a fourth grade student in their school had been killed. None of the students personally knew the fourth grader, but they became angry and vocal. They demanded to know why the child was in a situation where the accident could have occurred. They wanted to know where her parents were at the time of the accident. They questioned whether the child had been warned of the danger. They righteously discussed how the local city government could prevent this from happening again at the same site.

This age group will look for a meaning to the death just as intently as they look for the meaning to life. Astute teachers have the opportunity to honor their students' feelings and thus facilitate their healing.

The late adolescent or high school student's view of death is dependent on age, maturity and life experience. S/he carries this formed attitude into adulthood.

III

WHEN A STUDENT'S PARENT OR SIBLING DIES

Chapter III is divided into two sections, Section A for primary and middle school teachers, and Section B for high school teachers.

Each section will address what can be done the first school day after the death of a parent or sibling, and the second school day after the death of a parent or sibling. Attention will be given to the student whose parent or sibling has died, as well as the rest of the students in the classroom.

SECTION A - PRIMARY OR MIDDLE SCHOOL

FIRST SCHOOL DAY AFTER A PARENT OR SIBLING DIES

When the news comes into the office regarding the death of a parent or sibling of a student in your school, the principal should ask each teacher to briefly explain the facts concerning the death to his or her class. Since many students may have known the parent who died in the capacity of a scout leader or soccer coach, these students will have a need to express their loss.

After making the initial announcement, each teacher should determine the time needed for students to assimilate the news. Refer to the deceased by his/her name. "Mrs. Duwel died last night." Mrs. Duwel did not "pass on" or "go to live in Heaven" or "leave this mortal coil". We did not "lose" Mrs. Duwel. "Mrs. Duwel died." Allow the students to see an honest expression of your sadness, thereby giving them permission to acknowledge their own feelings.

11

The teacher can avoid undesirable behavior, such as indifference or crude humor, when the death is discussed by explaining to his/her students that often when we are frightened we tend to say cruel things to mask our fear. A friend related a painful incident from her childhood:

"I remember going outside to play the day after my mother died. The neighborhood children had broken up into two gangs, each of which occupied their own side of the street. When I arrived they were hurling insults back and forth. I automatically joined in the fun - fun, that is, until one of the enemy jumped up and hurled the ultimate insult... 'Your Mom is dead!' I was an adult before I realized his insult was yelled out of fear. It could have happened to him, too."

The sensitive teacher will be able to listen as students begin to label feelings such as anger, confusion, and fear. When confronted with the possibility of their own brother, sister or parent's death, students exhibit anxiety. When the class bully acts out, the creative teacher will respond by verbally acknowledging how frightened s/he must be feeling.

Encourage your students to talk with their own parent:

"After school today find some quiet time and ask your parents if you can tell them about what happened today. Ask if you can all sit down and talk about Mrs. Duwel."

OR

"Please don't minimize your need to talk through the feelings you are experiencing. Find someone at home with whom you can continue what we have begun here together."

You are not telling the student how s/he should feel, but you are suggesting that some concerns may need to be voiced, so his/her parent can provide the needed assurance.

In most cases, the child whose parent or sibling died will already be absent from the campus. If the grieving child is new to your school, we suggest that the principal contact the student's previous school in order for ex-teachers and old friends to respond appropriately.

A special responsibility falls on the teacher of the grieving child. His/her classmates will require more time for questions, introspection and sharing of concerns that first day. Depending on the age level and their familiarity with the person who died, individual needs will vary.

As an educator, you are familiar with the age level you teach, and will be prepared for the reactions you may hear from your students after you announce the death. For example, if you teach grades two or three, after their initial reactions, you will quite naturally be inundated with biological queries, some founded and some unfounded. The seven and eight year old may ask about decomposition, or continued growth of teeth and fingernails. Your answers should be given in the same manner you would explain any other natural fact of biology to this age group.

Different age levels and how they view death are explained in Chapter II, AGE LEVELS.

It will be difficult for the children to resume their class work, and it may be beneficial to read them an appropriate book from the school library that explains death to their age level. This story may provide the impetus for discussion. See Book List in Chapter IX.

We would encourage you to devote part of the school day to art work. Provide the children with materials and encourage them to make a personal card for their classmate and his/her family. You may review these cards when they are completed, but we doubt that you will find any of their sentiments inappropriate, because most young children have not yet been trained to substitute hurtful cliches for their true concerns and feelings.

Inform the children that you will deliver their cards to the family after school. Visiting the grieving is never easy; however, your willingness to act as a role model will imprint on the minds of your students that the grieving family's need for comfort, friendship and support far outweighs the family's need for privacy.

TEACHER INTERACTS WITH STUDENT WHOSE PARENT OR SIBLING HAS DIED

Interaction with the classroom teacher(s) and the rest of the faculty is expected and needed by the grieving student. It is normal for any child of school age to evaluate his/her own emotions, using the reactions of teachers as a measuring device. You can be quite sure the younger child is questioning if his/her teacher has been informed of the death. An immediate response can establish a trusting relationship.

Suggested Guidelines

Go to the home of the family, knowing the main purpose of your visit is to be with your student. Assure the young person of your concern. Give the student every opportunity to tell his/her version of how, why, when, and where the death occurred. Allow the young person to relate his/her feelings and concerns. For example, some misguided, well-meaning adult may have just told him, "Be brave, Cardell, you are the man of the family now that your father is gone." You can safely guarantee Cardell that he can remain an eleven-year-old fifth grader, and that he is not expected by those who love him to take the place of his father.

Be comfortable with silence. Your patience will give your student time to gather his/her thoughts and afford him/her a feeling of security. The child will benefit by your unhurried presence.

A young adult recounting the sudden death of her father commented, "The day my father suddenly died, people came to take care of the babies, and my mother's friends came to talk to

13

her, but I was nine years old and I didn't have anyone, so I sat in my room alone."

Promise the student you will have someone keep records of assignments and/or homework. Tests can be made up, and extended time for projects is acceptable. When the young person returns to school, leniency should be considered. As the teacher, you will set the limits, and these reasonable limits will act as a familiar framework the student will find reassuring.

Ask the student if s/he is involved in a sporting event, school play or special project during the next several days. Do not assume s/he wants to be excused from that activity. The child should be permitted to decide his/her degree of participation. It may be important for this young person to fulfill an obligation which can give him/her a sense of future normalcy.

You may hear the student say "It was my fault my mother died." With our adult reasoning, we know there is no possible way this student caused the parent's death, but s/he needs to work through that reasoning for him/herself. Immediately ask the child "Why do you think it was your fault? Your Daddy told me that your mother had a disease in her heart." The child may respond that s/he didn't clean his/her room or go to bed on time, or had been fighting with his/her sister, and that is why Mother died.

Assure the student that s/he did not cause the heart attack, and suggest s/he confirm this fact by talking with the surviving parent or the family's physician. A grieving child needs to hear in words that s/he does not have the power to bring about the death of anyone by thinking bad thoughts, through disobedience, or even by wishing it were so.

While you are with the student you may notice that his/her moods shift, that s/he may change the subject or announce that s/he is going outside to roller skate. Children at any age take as much as they can of a painful reality and then wisely take a break. Give the student time. Your body language and attentiveness will encourage openness, but the student will decide when and what s/he wishes to share.

If the student perceives you as a judgmental or smothering adult, you will lose his/her confidence. If the student perceives you as an active listener, the young person will be free to express his/her concerns.

SECOND SCHOOL DAY AFTER A PARENT OR SIBLING DIES

By the second day, either the classroom teacher or a representative of the school will have visited the student and his/her family. With permission from the family, we encourage you to share any new facts concerning the death. Never guess at what happened. If the death was determined to be suicide, call it a suicide. Do not judge, surmise, or make excuses.

If Emily's brother died of cancer, assure the students they cannot catch cancer from their friend, Emily, when she returns to school.

Don't give religious answers to medical questions asked by your students. For example, you won't want to say "Emily's brother died because God wanted him in Heaven." The fact is that "Emily's brother died because cancer cells invaded his vital organs." Assure the children that everyone does not die from cancer; in fact, cancer patients can be cured with treatment.

Assume your students will be attending the visitation and/or the funeral service for the parent or sibling of their classmate. Accurate information provided by the clergy or funeral director who will be officiating can diminish anxiety about what your students are about to experience. You may wish to send home a printed sheet including the full name of the person who died, and the date and time of funeral visitation and service. Word this announcement so parents realize their presence would be welcome and found to be supportive if it would be possible for them to attend.

Following a funeral service for the father of a fourth grader, a classmate was heard to comment to his friend, "My Mom and Dad wouldn't let me go. They said it would make me have nightmares. What did the body look like, anyway? Did he look like Freddy Krueger? Did everyone at the funeral scream and cry? I bet it was really gross!"

WHAT CHILDREN IMAGINE IS ALWAYS FAR WORSE THAN THE ACTUAL EXPERIENCE OF VIEWING THE DEAD BODY AT A MORTUARY. PARENTS OFTEN MISTAKENLY BELIEVE THEY CAN PROTECT THEIR CHILDREN FROM THE REALITY OF DEATH WHEN, IN FACT, THEY ARE MISSING THE OPPORTUNITY OF A TEACHABLE MOMENT.

SECTION B - HIGH SCHOOL

FIRST SCHOOL DAY AFTER A PARENT OR SIBLING DIES

When the news comes into the office regarding the death of a parent or sibling of a student in your school, the principal should ask each teacher to briefly explain the facts concerning the death to his/her class. In some cases, many students may have known the parent who died in the capacity of an intramural soccer coach or active school volunteer. These students will have a need to express their loss.

After making the initial announcement, each teacher should determine the time needed by his/her students to assimilate the news.

In this emergency situation, the school needs a capable, informed faculty member who will act as facilitator with those students who require special care. In most schools, this faculty member would be your school guidance counselor, or director of religious education. It is imperative that this facilitator be a person who is not uncomfortable listening to the grieving students. A designated area should be set aside for this purpose.

Refer to the deceased by his/her name. "Mr. Geiser died last night." Mr. Geiser did not "pass on", "expire ", "shuffle off this mortal coil", "go west", "go to the happy hunting grounds", or "join the choir invisible". We did not "lose" Mr. Geiser. "Mr. Geiser died."

Allow the students to see an honest expression of your sadness, thereby giving them permission to acknowledge their own feelings.

Explain that often when we are anxious and frightened, we tend to say cruel things to mask our fear. A friend related a painful incident at the time of his brother's death:

"I was a sophomore in high school when my brother was killed in an automobile accident. I remember being at the funeral home, and I overheard some guys from my school talking about me. One of them said "He's acting like a total gelhead! All he ever did with his brother was fight!" I was an adult before I realized that his remark was said out of fear. It could have been his brother who was killed."

The sensitive teacher will be able to listen as students begin to label feelings such as anger, confusion, and fear. Students of all ages, when confronted with the possibility of their own parents' or siblings' death, exhibit anxiety. When the class smart-mouth acts out, the creative teacher will respond by verbally acknowledging how frightened s/he must be feeling.

Encourage your students to talk with their own parents:

"Please don't minimize your need to talk through the feelings you are experiencing. Find someone at home with whom you can continue what we have begun here together."

You are not telling the student how s/he should feel, but you are suggesting that some concerns may need to be voiced, so parents or other significant adults can provide the needed assurance.

In most cases, the student whose parent or sibling died will be absent from the campus. If the grieving student is new to your school, we advise the principal to contact the student's previous school in order for ex-teachers and old friends to respond appropriately.

After the announcement of the death, there may be some students who cannot continue to attend class. In the past, one student may have experienced the death of his/her own

16

parent. Another student may have been close to the family. These particular students would be unable to concentrate on any class work, and should be given a hall pass and directed to join the counselor and the other grieving students in the designated area.

This special environment will provide the opportunity for these young people to talk through their pain and concern. Art materials can be made available to those students who have difficulty expressing themselves verbally. Their silent creations of color and shape will speak their fear, their pain, and their grief. Sharing their drawings can be a comfortable way of initiating discussion. Other students can design a sympathy card to be taken to the family.

The teachers who staff the safe place during the first day serve as exemplary role models. The students will witness their teacher's grief, concern and awkwardness as they all discuss the death. By observing the healthy emotional reactions of their teacher or counselor, the students will feel more secure as they begin to explore their initial grief reactions.

Students who are friends of the family members should be encouraged to go to the home of their fellow student, or send art work, a brief personal note, a flower, or some other expression of their concern.

Inform your students that you will hand-deliver their cards to the family after school if they are unable to do so. Visiting the grieving is never easy; however your willingness to act as a role model will imprint on the minds of your students that the grieving family's need for comfort, friendship, and support far outweighs the family's need for privacy.

TEACHER INTERACTS WITH STUDENT WHOSE PARENT OR SIBLING HAS DIED

Interaction with the classroom teachers and the rest of the faculty is expected and needed by the grieving student. It is normal for any high school age young person to evaluate his/her own emotions using the reactions of teachers as a measuring device. The student will be relieved that the teacher, the guidance counselor, and/or the principal realize the magnitude of his/her loss. An immediate response can establish a trusting relationship.

Suggested Guidelines

The faculty member who has the best rapport with the grieving student should go to the home of the family. Know that the main purpose of your visit is to be with your student. Assure the young person of your concern. Give the student every opportunity to tell his/her version of how, why, when, and where the death occurred. Allow the student to relate his/

her feelings and concerns. For example, some misguided, well meaning adult may have just told him, "Be brave Colin. You are the man of the family now that your father is gone." You can safely guarantee Colin that he can remain a seventeen-year-old junior, and that he is not expected to take the place of his father.

Be comfortable with silence. Your patience will give your student time to gather his/her thoughts and afford him/her a feeling of security. The student will benefit by your unhurried presence.

A young adult recounting the death of her brother commented, "The day my brother died, I wasn't allowed to be with my Mom and Dad. I wasn't allowed to use the phone, and I heard my aunt tell my friends that it wasn't a good time to come over. I was fourteen years old, and I was angry and scared. The last thing I wanted was to be alone. I needed someone to come just for me."

Promise the student you will have someone keep records of assignments and/or homework. Tests can be made up, and extended time for projects is acceptable. When the young person returns to school, leniency should be considered. As the teacher, you will set the limits, and these reasonable limits will act as a familiar framework the student will find reassuring.

Ask the student if s/he is involved in a sporting event, school play or special project during the next several days. Do not assume s/he wants to be excused from that activity. The young person should be permitted to decide his/her degree of participation. It may be important for this young person to fulfill an obligation which can give him/her a sense of future normalcy.

You may hear the student say "It was my fault my mother died. "With our adult reasoning, we know there is no possible way the young person caused the parent's death, but s/he needs to work through that reasoning for himself/herself. Immediately ask the student "Why do you think it was your fault? Your father told me she had a heart attack." Your student may respond "I had the car last night and after work I stopped by Ida's house. When I got home, Mother was worried, and had waited up for me. I know it's my fault she had the heart attack this morning."

Assure the student that s/he did not cause the heart attack, and suggest s/he confirm this fact by talking with the surviving parent or the family's physician. A grieving young person needs to hear in words that s/he does not have the power to bring about the death of anyone by thinking bad thoughts, through disobedience, or even by wishing it were so.

While you are with your student you may notice that his/her moods shift, that s/he may change the subject, stare at the TV, or announce that s/he is going to go work out. Give the student time. Your body language and attentiveness will encourage openness, but the student will decide when, and what s/he wishes to share.

If the student perceives you as a judgmental or smothering adult, you will lose his/her confidence. If the student perceives you as an active listener, the young person will be free to express his/her concerns.

SECOND SCHOOL DAY AFTER A PARENT OR SIBLING DIES

By the second day, either the classroom teacher or a representative of the school will have visited the student and his/her family. With permission from the family, we encourage you to share any new facts concerning the death. Never guess at what happened. If the death was determined to be suicide, call it a suicide. Do not judge, surmise, or make excuses.

If Sterling's sister died of cancer, assure the students they cannot catch cancer from their friend, Sterling, when he returns to school.

Don't give religious answers to medical questions asked by your students. For example, you won't want to say "Sterling's sister died because God wanted her in Heaven." The fact is that "Sterling's sister died because cancer cells invaded her vital organs." Assure the young people that everyone does not die from cancer; in fact, cancer patients can be cured with treatment.

Assume your students will be attending the visitation and/or the funeral service for the parent or sibling of their fellow student. Accurate information, provided by the clergy or funeral director who will be officiating, can diminish anxiety about what your students are about to experience. You may wish to send home a printed sheet including the full name of the person who died, and the date and time of funeral visitation and service. Word this announcement so parents realize their presence would be welcome and found to be supportive.

Following a funeral service for a seventeen-year-old killed in an accident, a mother of two teenagers was heard to lament as she left the church, "This funeral has given me a feeling of peace...a sense of closure. I only wish I had not discouraged my daughters from being here...I thought I was protecting them."

WE CANNOT PROTECT OUR YOUNG FROM THE PAINFUL REALITIES OF LIFE; ATTEMPTING TO DO SO INHIBITS GROWTH.

IV

WHEN A STUDENT IN YOUR SCHOOL DIES

This chapter is divided into two sections, one for primary and middle school teachers, and one for high school teachers. Each section will address what can be done the first school day after the death of a student, and the second school day after the death of a student.

When one of your students dies, we wish we could tell you that some talented, capable person will walk into your classroom and handle the situation. The hard, cold fact is you are the best person for this uncomfortable task.

Often, students resent an outside professional coming into their world at this most vulnerable time. You will have the support of your principal, your guidance counselor, your school psychologist, and your fellow teachers. It is imperative that you work as a team. As a teacher, you will be available in the months ahead when the professional is gone and your students need a resource. Because of your interaction at this critical time, the time of a death, the students will perceive you as someone who realizes what they are experiencing.

Because you are familiar with the history of your students (parent recently died, sibling has terminal illness, student has experienced the death of another young friend) you will instinctively watch for a resurgence of that student's grief.

Be prepared to observe students crying and holding on to each other in the halls. In the classroom setting, it is important to acknowledge the death that has occurred, and provide time for discussion if needed. The mistake which would have the longest and most negative effect on your students would be ignoring the death and/or proceeding with "class as normal".

Often a teacher will assume his/her class has no need to discuss the death of a student from another grade level. We only ask that you present the students with the opportunity to talk. In the following narrations, the teachers were not anticipating the reactions which occurred:

Natalie, a sixth grader, asked to be excused from class. An announcement had been read explaining that Amanda, a fourth grader, had been killed the night before. The class discussed the tragedy for a time and then began the day's work. Natalie had not made any contributions to the discussion, yet the teacher could see her pain and concern, so he excused her to talk with the bereavement specialist present in the school that day. The teacher was not aware that Natalie had been in a car pool with Amanda for three years. Natalie had an affection for Amanda, a big sister - little sister relationship. She needed to talk and tell stories of little Amanda, the kid who always stepped on the back of her shoe as she slid out of the car each morning. Natalie needed to be with others who knew Amanda.

We discourage you from verbalizing any opinions on a cause of death. No "probably" or "maybe".

The second grade teacher was very nervous at the thought of helping her class understand how a third grader had died after a fall down a hillside in the neighborhood park. She was prepared to read the statement written by the principal and not elaborate. After reading the statement to her young students they began to propose theories. There were multiple imagined scenarios about Amanda's accident. The parents' attempts to find a reason for Amanda's death were echoed in the school children's words, "If only…".

The teacher panicked, realizing she had to respond to each theory. Young second grader, Justin, came to her rescue by announcing in his eight-year-old voice, " You are all wrong! My dad is a fireman and he was there." Justin explained in detail how and where Amanda had fallen. He included all the emergency efforts that were employed to no avail. He concluded with the words "It was an accident. Nobody could help, they tried. The fact of life is: Amanda is dead." The students were satisfied, and the teacher was relieved.

In the same school, an older class of students reacted differently to the same death…

A seventh grade math teacher came into the faculty lounge and sighed, "You will never believe what I just went through! None of my students even knew Amanda. I thought reading the announcement would be sufficient, but I ended up with a room full of righteous adolescents demanding to know "Where were her parents?"… "Why didn't the park board close off that hill if it was dangerous?"… "Are there barriers now so another child is not hurt or killed?" Her students had a need to vent.

Most students' needs and issues will vary depending upon their maturity. When a student dies, the entire student body and faculty are affected. The following guidelines presented may assist you and your students at a time of pain and confusion.

SECTION A - PRIMARY OR MIDDLE SCHOOL

FIRST SCHOOL DAY AFTER A STUDENT DIES

The following is a sample directive prepared by the principal for teachers in a primary or middle school situation:

SAINT ZITA SCHOOL   Tuesday, February 21, 1989
RE: Death of Sebastian Greer (fifth grade) - February 20, 1989
Recognizing that we may not know the relationship Sebastian had with individual students on other grade levels, you will need to be observant. The fifth grade students will remain together for the day, and class work will resume at the discretion of the fifth grade teachers. If any student in any grade indicates the need for individual help, please have him/her escorted to the office. Dorothea Breeden (school secretary) will make arrangements for the student to see Claire Gelden (principal), Jeremy Chamber (director of religious education), Meredith Sherrer (school district psychologist), or Zach Morrison (bereavement specialist).

1. Each teacher will read the following statement of facts to his/her class:

    Last night your parents received a phone call from your room parent, telling them the sad news that Sebastian Greer had an accident and died. Mrs. Gelden went to Sebastian's home Monday evening following the news of his death. Mr. & Mrs. Greer asked her to bring the following information to you: After school yesterday, Sebastian rode his bike to his cousin's house on Telegraph Road. When Waller Creek was frozen, Sebastian would walk across it to his tree house instead of going all the way to Bonne Terre Bridge. His cousin, Cecil, saw Sebastian leave his bike in the driveway at 3:15 P.M. and head for the creek. Cecil and his friend, Jimmy, were working on a car. About 5:00 P.M., Cecil noticed a snow storm moving into the area, so they walked down to the creek to warn Sebastian. Cecil found Sebastian face-down in the creek. He immediately began C.P.R. Jimmy ran back to the house and called 911. Paramedics arrived, but nothing could be done. Sebastian was dead. There was a lump on his forehead. The authorities said he slipped, hit his head, became unconscious, and fell face-down into the creek, where he drowned.

2. Each teacher will decide the amount of time needed to field questions and listen to feelings. Only after needs have been met should class work resume.

    Fifth grade teachers may elect to permit students to do artwork, music, or create a card for the family. As a class, they may write memories of Sebastian to be taken later to the family.

3. Please do not disguise your sorrow. It is good to share your sadness with the children. Don't be afraid of your tears or theirs.

4. Some of the older students may question "Why did he go down there alone?" "Why didn't his cousin warn him of the melting ice?" "Why did his parents let him build a treehouse so near the creek?" It is not unusual for students this age to become self-righteous.

5. Do not lecture. This is not the time to review the rules for safe play.

6. Do not give religious answers to medical questions. Sebastian did not die because God wanted him in Heaven. Sebastian died because his lungs filled with water, and were deprived of oxygen. He could not breathe.

7. You may hear the question "Why did it happen?", and the statement "It isn't fair!". Your students will appreciate your honesty in saying "I don't know why it happened. It just did.", or "You are right. It isn't fair." And "No, this wasn't God's Will".

8. Relate only known facts. Do not draw your own conclusions. Do not make judgment calls. If you are unsure how to respond to a question, don't guess. Tell the students you will find the answer for them, or have the student talk with Claire, Jeremy, Meredith, or Zach.

9. Tell the students "Sometimes when we are frightened or scared, we cover up our fear by saying cruel things or making fun of those who are upset. So when you see someone who is being mean, you will know they are really frightened inside."

10. Assure your students that it is highly unusual for young people to die.

11. Issues which may arise:

    "Maybe Sebastian was not your good friend - that's okay."

    Students may express feelings of guilt because they recently had an argument or a fight with Sebastian. If they confide in you the details of the argument, listen, and assure them if they had had the opportunity they could have resolved their differences.

    Students may be angry with other students or teachers talking and laughing in the halls as if nothing happened. "How can they be so happy when I feel so bad?" Maybe they did not know Sebastian, or perhaps they are recalling a funny, happy time with Sebastian or, unfortunately, some people are just insensitive.

12. Information:

    If a parent shows up at your classroom, direct them to the office.

    The eighth grade field trip on Friday, February 24, to the Natural History Museum, will take place as scheduled.

    Greg (librarian) will pull books on grieving - he can advise on age level.

    All classes may plan an impromptu prayer service in class. Claire, along with the fifth graders and their teachers, will plan an all-school memorial service.

    A letter will be sent home with each student from Claire's office stating facts, Sebastian's full name, family address, date and time of visitation, and funeral Mass. Assume the children will go to both, but give no directives. The wording will encourage the parents to attend with their children if possible.

SECOND SCHOOL DAY AFTER A STUDENT DIES

During the first few days after the death of a student, the faculty will most likely be guilty of acts of omission rather than commission. In the role of teacher, you may be so organized and goal oriented that you overlook the needs of siblings, classmates, and those students who will be attending the funeral formalities.

Siblings

Often siblings will return to school the day following the death, and before the day of the funeral service; this is a personal decision. These siblings have a need to be where they feel most comfortable, and you will find that when the initial needs of all the teachers and students have been met, they are better prepared to surround the grieving siblings with a comfortable, safe, natural environment.

Especially in a large school, make sure ALL the teachers are aware that the sibling has returned to the school building. Be advised that these returning siblings have instantly acquired a phenomenal penchant for hearing beyond the normal scope. Siblings have related overhearing cold, crass comments made by teachers who thought they were well out of hearing range.

Classmates

On the second day after the death, the fellow students in the class of the deceased child may need a more-detailed explanation than was given the first day.

If... Eric died of heart failure, your best recourse would be to call in a health professional such as a physician or nurse who could supply diagrams, pictures of organs, and explanations of the normal workings of the heart. The professional could field questions and assure the students that "Eric was born with a defect in his heart. This problem is very unusual. This will not happen to your heart. This is how the doctors tried to repair Eric's heart."

If... Betsy died of a terminal illness, we would hope that the class had been made aware of and discussed Betsy's illness. With the parents permission, professionals from a Hospice or children's medical center would have been brought in to answer concerns of her classmates before the death. If this was not done, the students will need a medical explanation, suitable to their grade level, of the cause of death. In this situation we urge you to contact a health professional. The students need to understand that the disease which killed Betsy is not catching.

If... Amanda died in the emergency room after a fall, the students and faculty will require accurate information. Someone should visit the school, and explain the facts. This spokesperson should be selected by the family. They may suggest a family representative, a school administrator, one of the responding paramedics, police personnel at the scene, or a representative from the emergency room who was present at the time Amanda was brought into the hospital.

An eyewitness, or a professional, can assure the students that their classmate was cared for with respect and gentleness. S/he may be able to report that Amanda was not conscious or was in no pain. S/he can assure the students that the physicians employed all reasonable medical intervention to sustain life.

Students who will attend funeral formalities

At some time during this day, explain in detail what the students will see or hear at the mortuary, funeral service, and cemetery. Fear of the unknown can provoke inappropriate behavior in any of us. By previewing the new experience, the students will see their participation as less threatening.

Before school dismissal, students should be given written information regarding the time and location of the visitation at the funeral home, the burial service planned, and the cemetery committal. Your positive attitude regarding their attending these events will encourage them to participate.

SAINT ZITA SCHOOL

803 LeMay Ferry Road, St. Louis, Missouri

TO: Parents of children attending St. Zita School

FROM: Office of the Principal   DATE: February 21, 1989

Sebastian Greer, fifth grade, died Monday, February 20, 1989. Sebastian attempted to cross Waller Creek (on the way to his tree house) when he slipped, hit his head, and fell face-down in the water. Rescue attempts by paramedics were employed. He was pronounced dead at the scene. Sebastian is the son of Benedict and Rachael Greer, of 628 Aleghaney Drive.

Cecil Bockenkamp, Sebastian's cousin, who was at the scene of the accident, spoke to the fifth grade classes this morning.

Dr. Meredith Sherrer, School District Psychologist, Claire Gelden, Principal, Jeremy Chamber, Dir. of Religious Education, and Zach Morrison, Bereavement Specialist, have been available to those students who had questions or just wanted to talk.

A memorial will be decided upon by the fifth grade as a class, and all other students will be invited to participate.

VISITATION: Thursday, February 23, 8:30-10:30 A.M., Errun & Yornoc Funeral Home 803 Morris Avenue

FUNERAL SERVICE: Saint Zita Church
                    Thursday, February 23, 11:00 A.M.

Students, grades five through eight, are invited to attend the funeral service in church at the request of the Greer family.

Students, grades one through four, will be excused to attend the funeral service with their parent(s). Please advise teacher in writing.

Parents, we encourage you, if at all possible, to attend both the visitation and the funeral mass with your child. When the class enters the church, your child can be excused to sit with you.

━━━

My child _____ will be attending the visitation for Sebastian Greer, on Thursday February 23 , 1989. I understand I am responsible for providing transportation both to and from the funeral home. I will have my child back to his/her homeroom by 10:30 A.M.
Parent Signature: _____

SECTION B - HIGH SCHOOL

FIRST SCHOOL DAY AFTER A STUDENT DIES

It is the principal's responsibility to convene ALL faculty and staff prior to the start of the school day. If feasible, arrangements should be made for a school district psychologist and/or bereavement specialist to be present to field the questions of the teachers. To eliminate misunderstandings, the faculty and staff, as a group, should read through and discuss a printed statement of the known facts and suggestions prepared by the principal.

The following is a sample directive for a high school situation:

PEABODY HIGH SCHOOL   Tuesday, September 5, 1989
RE: Death of Anne Singleton (junior) - September 4, 1989

Recognizing that we may not know the relationship Anne had with individual students on other grade levels, you will need to be observant. Permit those students who were close to Anne to remain together for the day - they need each other. Room 404 will be set aside for these grieving students. Brian Melscher (school counselor) will cover the room all day. Students will be required to have a Hall Pass. If a student in your classroom indicates the need for individual help, please have someone escort him/her to the office. Bonnie Bays (school secretary) will make arrangements for the student to see Adam

Richards (principal), Brian Melscher (school counselor), Diane Brendan (school district psychologist), or Gabrielle Daniels (bereavement specialist).

1. Homeroom will be extended this morning. Each teacher will read the following statement of facts to his/her class:

   "Last night, Mr. Richards was at the hospital with Mr. and Mrs. Singleton and Anne's brother, Paul, and her sister, Maureen. They relayed the following information: Students, Polly Lewis and Patricia Ebly, accompanied the Singleton family to Lake Edmonde for Labor Day weekend. Monday, the young people went sailing, and returned to the cottage about 5:00 P.M. Anne told Polly and Patricia she was walking into the village to pick up a video for later that night. At 5:40 P.M., the constable arrived at the cottage to inform them that Anne had been hit by a car and was seriously hurt. Paramedics transported her to Malachy Hospital. Anne was pronounced dead at 7:15 P.M. Authorities arrested a Lake Edmond resident, and charged him with manslaughter, and driving under the influence of drugs and/or alcohol."

2. Each teacher will decide the amount of time needed to field questions and listen to feelings.

3. Please don't disguise your sorrow. If you are sad, tell them. Don't be afraid of your tears or theirs.

4. Many of your students will display anger at the driver of the car that killed Anne. Their anger is justified. Explore with the students constructive ways to vent that anger.

5. Do not lecture. This is not the time to review defensive driving techniques, or pontificate on drinking and driving.

6. Do not give religious answers to medical questions. Anne did not die because God wanted her in Heaven. Anne died because she was hit by a car, her chest was crushed and her lungs were deprived of oxygen.

7. You may hear the question, "Why did it happen?", and the statement, "It isn't fair!". Your students will appreciate your honesty in saying, "I don't know why it happened. It just did.", or "You're right, it isn't fair." And "No, this wasn't God's Will'."

8. Relate only known facts. Do not draw your own conclusions. Do not make judgment calls. If you are unsure how to respond to a question, don't guess. Tell the students you will find the answer for them, or have the student talk with Adam, Diane, Brian or Gabriel.

9. Be patient with your students. Acknowledge their fears. Remind them that they may observe the most frightened classmate among them masking his fear with cruel or macabre remarks.

10. Assure your students that it is highly unusual for young people to die. Even a casual acquaintance of Anne may react more strongly than we might anticipate. The student's vulnerability to death has been harshly exposed.

11. Issues which may arise:

"Maybe Anne was not your good friend - that's okay."

Students may express feelings of guilt because they recently had an argument with Anne. If they confide in you the details of the argument, listen, and assure them, if they had had the opportunity, they could have resolved their differences.

Students may be angry with other students or teachers talking and laughing in the halls as if nothing happened. "How can they be so happy when I am so devastated?" Assure your students that those laughing may never have known Anne, or perhaps they are recalling a funny incident involving Anne, or perhaps they are frightened and don't know how to deal with her death.

12. Information:

Report cards will still be distributed on Friday.

Contact Ben Matthews, Room 241, Anne's homeroom teacher, who will collect all of Anne's papers, art work, tests, etc. Don't throw ANYTHING away. Ben will deliver all these things to the family. Polly Lewis and Patricia Ebly have been given permission to clean out Anne's locker.

Susan Leander, who teaches the American Writers class to juniors, will make contact with all junior level students, and form a team of Anne's friends to coordinate a program to be held in the auditorium Wednesday afternoon, 1:30 P.M. This same group will talk over long range plans for a memorial to Anne. Please send any recommendations and/or suggestions you may have regarding the above to Susan.

Information sheets will be available in the Main Office tomorrow. The sheet will include Anne's full name, cause of death, family address, date and time of the funeral visitation and service. The bottom half of this sheet will contain a permission slip to be used by those who will be attending the funeral. Assume students will be attending visitation and/or service, but give no directives.

Gabrielle Daniels, bereavement specialist, will be in the Faculty Lounge until 1:30 P.M., if you want to touch base with her during your free period.

SECOND SCHOOL DAY AFTER A STUDENT DIES

During the first few days after the death of a student, the faculty will most likely be guilty of acts of omission rather than commission. In the role of teacher, you may be so organized and goal oriented that you overlook the needs of siblings, fellow students, faculty and those students who will be attending the funeral formalities.

Siblings

Often siblings will return to school the day following the death, and before the day of the funeral service; this is a personal decision. These siblings have a need to be where they feel most comfortable, and you will find that when the initial needs of all the teachers and students have been met, they will be better prepared to surround the grieving siblings with a comfortable, safe, natural environment.

Especially in a large school, make sure ALL the teachers are aware that the sibling has returned to the school building. Be advised that these returning siblings have instantly acquired a phenomenal penchant for hearing beyond the normal scope. Siblings have related overhearing cold, crass comments made by teachers and fellow students who thought they were well out of hearing range.

Fellow Students

On the second day after the death, the fellow students in the class of the deceased young person may need a more-detailed explanation than was given the first day.

If... Eric died of heart failure, your best recourse would be to call in a health professional such as a physician or nurse who could supply diagrams, pictures of organs, and explanations of the normal workings of the heart. The professional could field questions and assure the students that "Eric was born with a severe heart defect, which is very unusual. The doctor tried to correct the problem, but the surgery was unsuccessful."

If... Betsy died of a terminal illness, we would hope that the class had been made aware of and discussed Betsy's illness. With the family's permission, professionals from a Hospice or the local medical center would have been brought in to answer concerns of her fellow students before the death. If this was not done, the students will need a medical explanation of the cause of death. In this situation, we urge you to contact a health professional. The students need to understand that the disease that killed Betsy is not contagious.

If... Anne died in the emergency room after being involved in a traffic accident, the students and faculty will require accurate information. Someone should visit the school, and explain the facts. This spokesperson should be selected by the family. They may suggest a family representative, a school administrator, one of the responding paramedics, police personnel at the scene, or a representative from the emergency room who was present at the time Anne was brought into the hospital.

An eye witness or a professional can assure the students that their fellow student was cared for with respect and gentleness. S/he may be able to report that Anne was not conscious or was in no pain. S/he can assure the students that the physicians employed all reasonable medical intervention to sustain life.

Students who will attend funeral formalities

At some time during the day, someone needs to explain in detail what the students will see or hear at the mortuary, funeral service and cemetery. Fear of the unknown can provoke inappropriate behavior in any of us. By previewing the new experience, the students will see their participation as less threatening.

According to its size, each school needs to determine the best way of conveying this information to its students. It is a shame when young people miss the opportunity to support their fellow student because of poor communication.

Options

Homeroom Teachers could convey information during homeroom.

In a religious school, the information could be conveyed during a religion period.

In a private school, the information could be conveyed in an all-school assembly.

In a large high school, an announcement could be made and the guidance counselors could meet during lunch mods with those students planning to attend the visitation or funeral service.

Before school dismissal this second day, students could pick up a printed sheet stating the time and location of the visitation at the funeral home, the burial service planned, and the cemetery committal. A permission slip to be signed by the parent would be included.

The faculty's positive attitude regarding attendance at these events will encourage the students to participate.

V

WHEN SUICIDE HAPPENS

When a person completes suicide, society's natural reaction is to avoid the survivors. It makes us uncomfortable to place the family in a situation where they would have to admit someone they loved took his/her own life. This protective attitude isolates them from help. We have all grown up with learned prejudices toward self-execution, related directly to our environmental and religious backgrounds.

Before you find yourself in a situation where you must address the topic of suicide, you may wish to consider the following responses:

IN THE CASE OF A SUICIDE, I WOULD...

1. A. ...give the family complete privacy.
   B. ...call the family immediately and express the concern of the school and the classmates.

2. A. ...suggest to your students that they could embarrass the family by visiting at this time.
   B. ...encourage your students who are friends to visit their classmate, in the case of parent's suicide, and visit the parents, in the case of the a student's suicide. Their non-judgmental presence will bring the family comfort.

3. A. ...be vague about details of the death, and never use the word "suicide".
   B. ...if death was ruled a suicide, never lie or cover up the tragedy. The word is "suicide".

4. A. ...consider the preferred terminology as "S/he committed* suicide." (* to do; perpetrate, as a crime, sin, fault, folly or error.)
   B. ...consider the preferred terminology as "S/he completed* suicide." (* brought to an end or to a final or intended condition; concluded; completed.)

5. A. ...discourage your student from any arranged meeting with emergency medical

personnel, police, coroner or witness who discovered the body. These meetings will only cause anguish.

    B.   ...encourage the survivors to listen to any substantiated facts concerning the suicide.

6.   A.   ...suggest that siblings be sent to the home of a friend until after the funeral, or longer. Details of the suicide can often distress them.

    B.   ...impress upon those in charge how important it is for the siblings to remain with the immediate family. What a child imagines is always worse than the reality of what other family members are experiencing.

7.   A.   ...change the subject to happier times whenever a student implies that he/she should have been able to prevent the self-destruction.

    B.   ...concentrate on feelings, and allow students to recognize their guilt, or anger, or resentment.

8.   A.   ...suggest that photos and/or personal possessions of the deceased be put out of sight. You should then refrain from using the name of the deceased.

    B.   ...share photos and memories of the deceased. The students need to sort out their feelings for the deceased.

9.   A.   ...discourage the students from attending the visitation or the funeral out of respect for the family.

    B.   ...encourage your students to attend the visitation and/or funeral. Their attendance will be viewed by the surviving family as support from a caring community.

10.   A.   ...know that the survivors will not expect flowers or memorial contributions, considering the circumstances of death.

    B.   ...know that survivors need physical, outward signs of the friendship others felt for the deceased.

11.   A.   ...decide that it is too late to bring in outside professional help after a student or student's family member has completed suicide.

    B.   ...seek the help of mental health professionals, bereavement specialists or members of the local Survivors After Suicide support group and learn how to best help confused students.

The "A" statements are common stereotypical reactions. They are a result of misinformation passed down over the years. As you noticed, the preferred response is always listed as choice "B". The topics covered in the above statements were all based on comments shared with us by survivors after suicide.

The time for quality education on suicide is BEFORE the tragedy occurs. The teacher's best source of information would be <u>Survivors After Suicide</u> (listed in Resources, Chapter IX). It is generally thought that talking about suicide encourages young people to choose this option when, in fact, the potential suicide may be defused by a quality presentation.

Class discussion groups in high schools usually reveal that someone the students know has threatened, attempted, or at least considered killing her/himself. Peer counseling programs have also been found to be very effective. Following is dialogue from one such session:

During a group discussion in a small high school a young woman blandly admitted, "I hate school and I really don't have any reason to get up in the morning." The fifteen year old redhead across the table shot back at her, "I know what you mean. My mom died when I was twelve, my father is never around, and my boyfriend was killed in an accident last year. I thought about suicide. Then I decided age sixteen has got to be better, and I'm not going to cheat myself out of finding out!"

Students balk at being disloyal to a friend who has confided in them. The students need to be aware of outside resources, and they need permission to break the iron code of silence when faced with a friend who is troubled and contemplating suicide. Encourage your students to call the local suicide hot line and ask for advice on how to respond to a friend talking about suicide. Students and teachers must also realize they do not have the power to cause another person to complete suicide nor have they the power to continually prevent another person from completing suicide.

A major concern of educators is how to recognize the student who is considering suicide as an option. We suggest an in-service for teachers presented by local mental health services, those professionals who staff the suicide hot line in your area, or members of the Survivors After Suicide support group.

When a student in your school completes suicide, the entire school community is affected. Meeting the needs of all is an overwhelming task that must be undertaken immediately.

After the suicide of a student, the faculty and fellow students will ask themselves many questions:

"Why couldn't he trust me enough to talk to me? I feel betrayed!"

"How could he be so stupid as to chose suicide as a way out? I am angry and I resent what he did!"

"Why didn't I go to his parents, or anyone who could have intervened? I knew he was depressed!"

"If he had everything going for him and he still decided to kill himself - how am I going to make it? I am scared!"

"Why didn't he at least say goodbye? I hate him for not asking for help!"

At the time of a suicide, the school should immediately seek the assistance of trained members of a suicide support agency to field questions and help the faculty identify other students who may require intervention at this time of crisis.

By addressing the suicide immediately, the school breaks the code of silence and sets the scene for the teachers to do realistic follow up.

The following example relates how one teacher acknowledged the fear and confusion that plagued some of his students following a suicide:

A student from the junior class in a large high school had completed suicide. In the months following the tragedy, the junior level history teacher used many examples in his lessons to point out the fact that all persons have choices to make. The teacher went out of his way to explain how in most situations the solutions to problems were not evident. The historical character had to study contradictory facts and seek out people who could objectively illuminate the options available.

This wise history teacher did not dwell on the actual suicide; instead he bolstered the self-esteem of the survivors of the suicide. In his classroom, he presented life as a realistic experience with successes and failures. He talked about doors instead of brick walls. Without preaching, he clearly presented survival techniques to his students in his daily history lessons.

Both teachers and students must realize they are not responsible for the actions of another person, but they can be responsible to another person by seeking intervention when it is indicated.

VI

ATTENDING THE VISITATION, FUNERAL SERVICE AND CEMETERY PROCEEDINGS

TERMINOLOGY

Following is a list of terms you will be using with your students. The definitions are basic in order to be easily used with the young child, and yet enable you to elaborate on the base definition to meet the needs of more mature students.

autopsy:
an examination of the organs and tissues of the dead body to determine cause of death. This is done by a special doctor called a pathologist.

burial:
placement of the casket or urn into the ground.

burial vault:
a container made of concrete or steel, which is designed to hold up the weight of the earth, and to protect the casket.

casket:
a container designed to hold a body for viewing and burial. At the time of burial, the casket has a lid to protect the body.

cemetery:
designated area of ground reserved for the burial of a body into the grave (or ground) prepared for it.

columbarium:
a type of mausoleum, a wall with niches to retain urns.

condolence:
an expression of sadness, loss and concern for a person who is grieving a death.

cremate:
the burning of a dead body to bone residue in a retort (special furnace), located in a crematory.

dead:
when life stops. There is no longer brain activity. The heart does not beat. The lungs do not take in air. The body no longer feels heat, pain or cold.

embalm:
the use of chemicals to disinfect, sanitize and temporarily preserve a dead body, so that the body can be present for the funeral rites.

funeral:
ceremony at the time of burial or cremation.

grave:	an open site in the earth prepared to receive a casket, or cremains.
grave liner:	a container made of concrete designed to hold up the weight of the earth.
grave marker:	each grave is marked with an engraved stone or metal plaque that includes information about that person who died. (Other acceptable terms: monument, or headstone.)
hearse:	a special vehicle designed to transport a dead body from one place to another. (Other acceptable terms: funeral coach or casket coach.)
Hospice:	an organization of nurses, doctors and other professionals who care for the terminally ill and deal with the counseling of family members.
interment:	placement of the casket containing the dead body into the space provided for it in a mausoleum, or a grave.
inurn:	to encase the cremated remains of a body in an urn.
mausoleum:	a building designed to permanently house a large number of caskets containing dead bodies. Each casket is placed in its own sealed crypt and labeled with a plaque which includes information about that person who died.
mortuary/ funeral home:	a place where the dead body is prepared and retained for viewing until the time of burial or cremation.
outer burial container:	a concrete or steel container required by the cemetery in which the casket is placed to prevent the grave from collapsing.
suicide:	when a person deliberately kills his/her own body; the killing of one's self on purpose.
terminal illness:	a sickness or disease that cannot be stopped or cured and, after a period of time, causes the very sick person's death.
urn:	a container that holds the cremated remains of the deceased following the cremation of a body.

TEACHER EXPLAINS MORTUARY TO STUDENTS

The physical act of visiting a special place where the body of a dead person can be viewed internalizes the fact that indeed this person is dead. Making closure is an important first step in the grief process. The effort one makes to put oneself in an uncomfortable situation is not lost on the family of the deceased. Being there is a visible sign of concern and support for the survivors. A visitor's presence, embrace or handshake is a simple expression of sympathy, and is a gesture the grieving will appreciate.

When a school-related death occurs, the teacher has a unique opportunity to open the doors of human compassion, a lesson students will draw upon their entire lives.

Before explaining to the students what they will encounter at the mortuary, have accurate information. Do not assume your personal knowledge of the funeral home, the funeral service, and the cemetery procedure is accurate. For example, in unusual situations the family may choose to have a closed casket at the funeral home.

Cultural background could alter the procedure at the funeral home: During the visitation honoring a Chinese/American, visitors approach the casket, light an incense stick and place it in a vase provided, or they may burn gifts of play money in a large copper urn because, as Chinese/Americans, they believe it will be real when it reaches the spirit world. Their funeral procession may include a band playing spirited hymns.

Please contact the funeral director in each situation to ascertain the particulars. The vocabulary and number of details you share with your students depends on the age level you are teaching. Do not rely solely on the following basic explanation:

A mortuary or funeral home

You should tell your students that the mortuary or funeral home is a building, often resembling a house, where the body is taken after death. A funeral director is chosen by the family to move the body to the funeral home. A funeral director is a person who attends mortuary school for many years to be trained to care for and prepare a body for burial, and learn how best to assist the family members of the deceased. "...Mr. Eggalp, of the Reyem Funeral Home is a mortician, and he will be preparing Olivia's body for the visitation."

A mortician cares for the body

The purpose of embalming is disinfection, sanitation and temporary preservation so that the body may be present for the funeral rites.

You should tell your students that the mortician will gently wash the body, comb the hair, apply some makeup, blush or lipstick to the face, and then carefully dress the body in clothing chosen by the family.

In all countries, for centuries, people have experienced the benefits of viewing the dead. Seeing the body confirms visually what we already know. The person who died no longer feels. The heart does not beat; the lungs do not take in air. S/he is dead.

The appearance of the body

You should tell your students that the body will be lying on a plush covered mattress in a wood or metal casket. There will be a small pillow placed under the head. The eyes of the person who died will be closed. The family may decide to have the funeral director put the glasses belonging to their loved one on his/her face because that is how friends remember him/her. The hands may be crossed or something special may be placed in the hands, such as flowers, a religious article, or, in the case of a child, you may see a blanket or stuffed animal. If someone were to touch the hands, they would feel hard and cold.

The visitation room

You should tell your students that when they walk into the foyer of the funeral home, there may be a book present where you can register your name. Later, this book is given to the family of the person who died. There may be memorial cards present indicating the wishes of the family regarding the destination of charitable contributions in the name of the deceased.

In the visitation room, which may resemble a living room or parlor in a private home, the casket will be on a platform so it is elevated off the floor. Some denominations may request a kneeler be present at the side of the casket. Visitors have the option of kneeling and silently praying for a moment or two, or pausing and then walking by the casket. Children should never be made to feel they must approach the casket. Allow each child to choose his/her own distance.

When you first enter the visitation area, you may hear soft music playing in the background, and you may notice the sweet smell of flowers. People will be quietly talking and some even crying because they are sad. People will be relating stories, and you may hear laughter. The casket may be surrounded by baskets of flowers sent by friends. There may be one large candle on a stand at the head of the casket. You may see a collage of mounted photographs of the person who died. The photographs help people recall memorable events in his/her life.

The appropriate behavior.

You should tell your students that while they are at the funeral home, the family of the deceased will usually form an informal receiving line, and you are welcome to greet any or all members to express your condolences. An expression of condolence may simply be a nod, eye contact, a handshake, or a hug. A condolence may include words which express your sadness and loss, and your concern for the survivors. It is appropriate and comforting to the survivors for people to:

1. Use the name of the deceased.
   "I met Molly when we were in gymnastics together."

2. Identify yourself.
   "I'm Saundra Angelo. I was Molly's locker partner last year."

3. Relate a positive incident you shared.
   "I'll always remember how Molly got everyone on the bus to sing when we went to State Finals."

While you are at the funeral home, the funeral director or a clergy person may conduct a service. Out of respect, everyone is quiet and attentive during this time.

We realize it is awkward and uncomfortable to go to the mortuary; the grieving family knows this and will remember and appreciate the effort you make. The dead cannot bury themselves. Our participation at the funeral home can be seen as a final act of friendship to the deceased, and a demonstration of our concern for the survivors.

TEACHER EXPLAINS FUNERAL SERVICE TO STUDENTS

Each of us is more comfortable in any social setting when we have been made familiar with the anticipated proceedings.

Before describing the funeral service or ceremony to your students regarding a specific denomination, you will need to contact the funeral director or minister scheduled to officiate. Your students will benefit by having accurate information.

Those officiating at the funeral service will appreciate being advised that young people will be present. Those planning the service can then be prepared to speak to the pain of the young mourners assembled.

The rite of burial varies, depending on local custom, denomination, cultural and/or ethnic backgrounds. One should note that there are no "rights" or "wrongs", simply differences. Often, there is variability of ritual within even a single denomination. People of all faiths seek to bury their dead with dignity, honor and sensitivity to the needs of survivors.

This section will cover three types of funeral services: Protestant, Jewish, and Roman Catholic. We wish to thank Rev. Donald Wells, Pastor, Mount Washington Presbyterian Church; Rev. Wendell E. Mettey, Senior Pastor, Montgomery Community Baptist Church; Rabbi Kathy Schwartz, Assistant Rabbi, K. K. Bene Israel/Rockdale Temple; and Rev. Steven Walter, Worship Director, Cincinnati Catholic Archdiocese, for their help in compiling this section.

PROTESTANT FUNERAL SERVICE
Wendell E. Mettey, Senior Pastor, Montgomery Community Baptist Church:

Generally speaking, there is no prescribed funeral service all Protestant clergy follow. Many clergy will use the recommended service of their denomination. Most services, however, are entirely at the discretion of the officiating clergy.

An important part in preparing the service is the consultation with the family of the deceased. This usually happens when the clergy visits the family of the deceased. At this time the family will give to the clergy favorite scripture, hymns, poems, etc. of the deceased. The clergy will then incorporate them into the service.

Most funeral services are held at the funeral home. The day of the service the funeral director will set up chairs, usually facing the casket. The clergy who is officiating will speak to those gathered from a lectern near the casket. The funeral director assists the clergy throughout the service.

The casket may be opened or closed depending upon the wishes of the family. An open casket places emphasis on the deceased, as s/he was known in life. The closed casket is a reminder that the deceased is no longer with us but has been raised to eternal life through Jesus Christ.

When the service is held in the church building, the opportunity for visitation with family members and viewing of the body may occur prior to the service. Usually the visitation will be the night before, at the funeral home. The day of the service, the funeral director will bring the deceased to the church building prior to the arrival of family and attending guests. As the guests arrive, they are seated in the sanctuary. The family waits until the service begins. The clergy may wear a robe or dark suit, and in some churches will precede the closed casket as it is brought in and positioned in the front of the sanctuary. The family follows and is seated in the front pews.

The contents of the service remain similar whether performed in the funeral home or the church sanctuary. One may participate in congregational singing, or a soloist selected by the family may perform musical selections. Scripture can be read from the Old Testament and New Testament. Poetry, or works written by friends or family members may be shared. A eulogy may be given, describing the accomplishments of the deceased, and a sermon delivered, based on the theme of Christian life and the promise of eternal life with God through Jesus Christ.

When the funeral home service is concluded, the funeral director invites those present to pay their final respects to the deceased. Some will file by the casket, say their silent goodbyes and leave the viewing room. The immediate family will have some private time, and be the last to leave.

At the conclusion of the church service, casket bearers will carry the casket to the hearse, preceded by the pastor and followed by the family and friends. The hearse will be the lead car in the procession from the funeral home or church to the burial ground. Anyone may go to the cemetery.

For people to take the time to go to the graveside service means a great deal to the family.

Rev. Donald Wells, Pastor, Mount Washington Presbyterian Church:

The Protestant funeral service is a service of variety. Some churches will have communion or the Lord's Supper during the service. You may find a standard liturgy, or worship service or you may discover a service that seems to be spontaneous. The service may be held in a local church, or in the funeral home. Yet in the midst of all of this variety, there are several things which are basic, and are included in most Protestant services.

In Protestant churches, the funeral is a service which witnesses to the resurrection. It proclaims the hope that God's love is stronger than death and can even overcome death. We also believe that the funeral service celebrates a person's life. It celebrates the good which s/he did, which celebrates God's love. The funeral service also acknowledges our feelings of loss, at our loved one's death. We cannot deny that the death of a loved one hurts. Each one of these elements has a necessary place in the service.

Usually the service will begin with a call to worship and prayer. This is to remind us that the funeral is a service of worship whether it takes place in a church or a funeral home.

Next will come readings from the Old and New Testament. From the Old Testament, the book of Psalms is frequently used because many of the Psalms acknowledge the reality of death and God's comfort even in the midst of death. Readings from the New Testament will usually focus on the resurrection and hope.

Sometimes a eulogy or summary of the person's life is given. This is done to help the loved ones celebrate the person's life, to acknowledge their accomplishments in life and to point to their humanness. Hopefully a good eulogy helps the loved ones to say, "Yes, that is the way s/he was."

Then comes a meditation or sermon. The length on this will vary from one service to another. A five or ten minute talk is seen as a meditation with a sermon usually being longer. The meditation is a time to acknowledge our loss and also to point at our hope.

After the meditation will be a prayer. This prayer may give thanks for the person's life, once again acknowledging our pain and asking for comfort for the person's loved ones. Quite often after the prayer will be the Lord's Prayer which is an opportunity for everyone to participate in the service. A Benediction may either be given at the close of the service or at the end of the graveside service.

Sometimes the casket is opened after the service, so that people may acknowledge their feelings toward the person and also acknowledge the reality of the death. Other services will end with the casket being closed and will focus on hope rather than viewing the body.

Normally the family and loved ones will accompany the casket to the graveside. There a short service is offered. This will consist of prayers, perhaps scripture, and will include words of committal. An example of words of committal would be "In sure and certain hope of the resurrection to eternal life we commend to Almighty God our brother/sister and we commit his/her body to the ground: earth to earth, ashes to ashes, dust to dust." This is still another way of admitting the reality of the death.

As the Protestant services vary so do some of the accompanying customs, from church to church and from different regions in the country. Often in the Northern area there will be a service of visitation so that friends can express their feelings of support to the family of the deceased. In the South usually the family will not be at the funeral home, but will receive friends at a dinner or luncheon after the service.

The funeral is a way of honoring the person's life and it is also for the living as a way of acknowledging their loss and to be reminded of the hope which we have in God's love and care.

JEWISH FUNERAL SERVICE
Rabbi Kathy Schwartz, Assistant Rabbi, K. K. Bene Israel/Rockdale Temple:

Judaism can be expressed in many different ways with either less emphasis or greater emphasis on the traditional Jewish legal conception. For the most part, the Jewish people are divided into a few major movements, reflecting basic philosophical differences.

Some Jews believe that the Holy Scriptures are the direct work of God through the hand of Moses and that later rabbinic interpretation is also reflective of the Will of God. These people are Orthodox Jews. Liberal Jews, on the other hand, generally do not believe that the Bible or its later interpretations consistently reflect the direct Will of God. For Liberal Jews, the traditions and customs of the Jewish people are of great importance, for they reflect the Jewish way of life. It should be understood that the following brief outline of the Jewish way in death and dying is written from the perspective of a Liberal Jew. Whenever possible, differences in practice will be noted.

Judaism recognizes two very important concepts relating to death. The first is that absolute respect must be given to the corpse. Many laws have been created to ensure this respect for the dead. Secondly, one of the most important commandments in Judaism is to comfort the mourner. The funeral ceremony and the grieving customs are based on these two concepts.

Upon hearing about the death of a loved one, the pious Jew will respond with the phrase "Blessed be God, the Judge of truth." Judaism separates the mourners into two distinct groups - immediate family and other loved ones and friends. The immediate family members include: father, mother, brother, sister, son, daughter, and spouse. The laws of mourning are followed by these members of the immediate family. Other extended family members and friends join the immediate family members at the funeral and provide support and comfort to the mourners.

Traditional Judaism opposes any type of incision made on the body of the deceased. Therefore, unless it is a medical necessity or required by state law, traditional Jews will not permit an autopsy or embalming of the body. The funeral will generally take place within three days of the death, and, until that time, the body will be refrigerated for preservation. The body, in traditional Judaism, is thoroughly washed and prepared by a group of Jewish volunteers who believe that such a task is a sacred duty. From the time of death until the funeral ceremony, traditional Jews do not leave the body alone. Judaism understands respect for the dead to suggest that at all times the casket should be closed.

Traditional Jews are buried in a white shroud with their prayer shawls. Orthodox Jews follow the custom of burying their dead in a simple pinewood coffin. These practices are followed because Jews believe that in death all people are equal. The wealthy, as well as the indigent, have access to these materials. Pinewood is used as it disintegrates quickly and thereby fulfills the Biblical injunction "..for dust you are, and to dust you shall return."(Genesis 3:19) All of these practices are followed as they fulfill the Jewish understanding of respect for the dead.

Upon entrance to a funeral ceremony, one would be encouraged to offer comfort to the bereaved. In general, the immediate family has gathered in a separate room to receive visitors. The Rabbi is often not present until ten to fifteen minutes before the ceremony. Most Rabbis will not wear their robes or prayer shawls at the funeral ceremony. They will be dressed in appropriate professional clothing. One may find that there will be a basket of skullcaps for the men to wear at the entrance of the funeral home. These caps, called either kippot (long o) or yarmulkes, are worn to show respect for God.

As the ceremony begins, one may see the immediate family members with a black ribbon attached to their lapel. Immediately prior to the ceremony , the ribbon is cut, symbolizing the mourner's inner feeling of a heart torn asunder. This practice is called "keriah" (literally meaning tearing). The funeral ceremony consists of several psalms, often including Psalm Twenty Three (The Lord is my shepherd, etc.), a eulogy, and a prayer suggesting that the soul of the deceased be bound up in the bonds of eternal life.

Appropriate and thematic poetry is often added to the ceremony. Rarely is there any music with the exception of the chanting of the prayers. The greatest portion of the funeral ceremony is dedicated to the eulogy.

The mourners and close friends then accompany the casket to the cemetery. (There is the option to have only a graveside ceremony.) At the cemetery a very brief service is held. The final prayer, called the Kaddish, praises God for the gift of life. It is suggested that even at this most trying time, the Jew should praise God, though the natural tendency may be to yell out in anger. The mourners may choose to leave the cemetery at this time. Traditional Jews will often remain for the lowering of the casket and, out of love for the deceased, they will choose to place the first few shovelfuls of dirt on the casket. Often, the mourners who are close friends or more distant family will form two lines through which the immediate family will be escorted to their cars.

In affirmation of life, the mourners (both the immediate family and friends) will gather at the home of one of the immediate family members. It is appropriate to bring gifts of food, and for the mourners to eat together. Despite the harshness of death, the nourishing of life is considered important. Often, hard boiled eggs will be among the foods that are served. The egg symbolizes the potential of life and its cyclical shape suggests that the life of the soul does not end.

In more traditional homes, one may find that the mirrors are covered and that shoes are removed at the entrance to the home. The initial period of grieving called "shiva" (meaning seven, referring to the upcoming seven days) has officially begun. During this time, the mourners who are members of the immediate family do not attend joyous events and, if possible, absent themselves from work or school. During this week of intense grieving, the mourners do not worry about their physical appearance and the men to not shave. In traditional homes the family will sit on low stools and refrain from use of radio or television as a means of enjoyment. Visitors will visit the family in the evening and join together in a prayer service. (Liberal Jews often observe these customs for a period of three days, rather than seven.) It is customary that the mourners attend Sabbath services at their synagogue during this week. During the service, the deceased's name is commemorated with the recitation of a prayer, thanking God for the gift of life.

The first thirty days after the death of a loved one are considered to be a time of moderate mourning. Traditional men will continue to refrain from shaving and the mourners will avoid joyous gatherings. They will, however, return to work or school and begin to live a normal life once again. Traditional Jews will attend synagogue services every day for an entire year after the death of a loved one. They do so in order to recite a prayer (the Kaddish) on behalf of the deceased, which can only be recited when a community of ten Jews is present. Liberal Jews will attend services on each of the four Sabbaths following the death.

On the anniversary of the death (called Yahrzeit), the immediate family members will light a memorial candle which lasts for twenty-four hours. They will also generally attend services on each subsequent anniversary of the death. Often, one year after the death, the family members will gather in a ceremony to unveil the tombstone. With the unveiling, the year of grieving has come to an end.

One additional custom which is followed by the vast majority of Liberal Jews, and some Orthodox Jews as well, is called "Yizkor" (a service of memorial). This service, which is very brief, occurs on the afternoon of the Day of Repentance (Yom Kippur) and during the morning service for each of the three pilgrimage festivals: The Feast of Tabernacles (Succot), Passover, and The Feast of Weeks (Shavuot). The names of all who have passed away during the prior year are recited during this brief service. The Yizkor Service provides one more opportunity for the bereaved to work through their grief.

ROMAN CATHOLIC FUNERAL RITES
Rev. Steven Walter, Worship Director, Cincinnati Catholic Archdiocese:

There is a variety of options commonly found in the various stages of a funeral as it is celebrated in the Roman Catholic Church. There are frequently three elements or times of prayer: The Vigil Service, the Funeral Mass, and the Burial. These three times of prayer may be modified or omitted based on the needs or desire of the family. Sometimes, for a variety of reasons, the Funeral Mass is replaced by a "Liturgy of the Word" either in Church or at the Funeral Home.

The Vigil or Wake Service
The visitation at the funeral home usually includes a prayer service. It is commonly referred to as a "Vigil" or a "Wake Service." While there is room for adaptation and variety in the contents of this service, it most frequently includes readings from the Bible, prayers, and hymns. Sometimes favorite prayers or hymns, either of the family or the person who has died will be included at this service at the funeral home.

The Mass of Christian Burial
The second element that is often part of the Roman Catholic Funeral is the Funeral Mass or "Mass of Christian Burial." It is, in structure and content, the same basic service that takes place in the Catholic Church every Sunday, and is the most important public prayer of the Church. For a Mass of Christian Burial there are some specific elements and prayers that are added because of the occasion and the faith of the Church which is being celebrated.

For this celebration, the family and friends of the deceased accompany the body in procession to the Church. The Funeral Mass must always take place in Church. The casket is closed, and the priest greets the family and the body at the door of the Church. The body of the deceased is sprinkled with holy water, recalling the person's baptism, and a large white cloth, called a pall, is placed on the casket. This pall is a reminder of the "baptismal garment" with which the deceased was clothed at baptism.

The priest and other ministers lead the procession up the center aisle of the church. The casket is given a place of honor in the church and near it is a large candle called a "Paschal Candle." This candle is a sign of Jesus Christ, who is risen from the dead, and who is "the Light of the world."

The Mass continues with a prayer and the reading of scripture. All sit for the readings from the Old Testament and from one of the New Testament Epistles. These readings are usually read by persons other than the priest. Sometimes family members of the deceased, or members of the parish will fulfill this role. When the gospel is read, all stand. The gospel is proclaimed by a deacon, or if there is no deacon, by the priest. It is followed by a homily (sermon) given by the deacon or priest. The focus of the homily is on the faith of the Church, especially our faith in Jesus who rose from the dead. The scripture readings just proclaimed will give further focus to the homily.

The homily is followed by a series of brief prayers, to which all present make a common response. These prayers are for the person who has died, his/her family, and the needs of the world in general. Usually a member of the congregation, other than the priest, will lead these prayers.

After the Intercessory Prayers, the Preparation of the Gifts and Altar takes place. Usually some of the family members bring forward bread and wine which will be used for the celebration of the Eucharist. After the altar table is set, the priest proclaims a long prayer in the name of all present. It is called the Eucharistic Prayer, and is a prayer of praise and thanks to God recalling the wonderful deeds God has done for his people throughout salvation history.

In preparation for communion, all pray together the Lord's Prayer. This is a prayer that asks for forgiveness, and for "our daily bread." This is followed by "The Sign of Peace," a gesture which acknowledges the presence and peace of Christ that is present among us.

When it is time for the distribution of communion, all baptized, practicing members of the Roman Catholic Church are welcome to approach the altar for the reception of communion. All others remain in their places. Often the priest will associate some other members of the assembly with himself in the distribution of communion. These persons have been specially trained and designated to do this beforehand.

After communion, the priest stands near the body of the deceased for the Prayers of Final Commendation. This usually consists of an invitation to pray, some silence, a hymn, and a final prayer. After these prayers, the service is ended. Usually, the congregation sings a hymn, while the family and the body of the deceased leave in a procession led by the priest and other ministers of the liturgy.

Some Additional Points of Information

At the Funeral Mass the priest wears vestments over his normal street clothes. The alb is a long white garment. It is a symbol of the white garment that we are clothed in at baptism. Over the alb he wears a stole, which is a narrow piece of cloth similar to a scarf. It is worn around the neck and falls almost to the floor. Over this is worn a chasuble. It is a large ample outer garment most commonly white at a funeral Mass. Purple or black are also colors that are permitted.

The priest may sometimes be accompanied by a deacon. The deacon fulfills a variety of functions in the liturgical celebration, including the reading of the gospel. The deacon wears an alb and stole, and sometimes a dalmatic. The stole of the deacon is worn over the left shoulder. The dalmatic is an outer garment similar in design to the chasuble, but with sleeves. The color of the deacon's stole and dalmatic matches that worn by the priest.

Servers or altar attendants are normally present to help the priest and deacon during the ceremony. They perform tasks such as carrying the cross, the candles, and incense in procession. They hold the book when he proclaims the prayers, carry the holy water, and help prepare the altar with gifts of bread and wine.

Other roles that may be filled by a variety of persons include Special Ministers of Communion, who help the priest and deacon in the distribution of communion to those present. Cantors or leaders of song, who may lead the assembly in the hymns and responses sung, as well as sing some solo parts of those songs when appropriate.

In a very real sense, the liturgy is celebrated by the entire assembly of persons gathered. There are specific roles and ministries, all of which are important and necessary for the proper celebration of the Funeral Mass. Those persons who perform a specific function, such as priest, reader, cantor, etc., do not celebrate the Mass for the people, but with them.

If the funeral is a military funeral and a flag drapes the casket, the flag is removed at the door of the church when the funeral pall is placed on the casket. The flag is then placed on the casket again at the door as the casket is carried in procession out of the church.

Liturgy of The Word

In some cases the Funeral Mass is replaced by a Liturgy of the Word. This may take place in church, or at the funeral home. A variety of reasons may lead to the decision not to celebrate the Funeral Mass. There are, for example, days like Good Friday on which a Funeral Mass is not permitted. The Liturgy of the Word would include elements described above for the Funeral Mass, such as the greeting of the body at the door, sprinkling with holy water and clothing with the pall, the proclamation of the scripture readings and homily, the intercessory prayers, and the prayers of the final commendation.

The Burial

The Burial Service or Committal Service takes place in the cemetery. Many Catholic Churches have adjacent cemeteries, and the procession out of church continues to the place of burial. In other circumstances, the casket and family and friends are transported by car to the cemetery. At the cemetery there are prayers for the deceased, prayers for the family and readings from the Bible. Sometimes hymns are sung. The services take place at the grave or perhaps in a chapel in the cemetery.

Local custom dictates what may occur before or after the funeral service. Patriotic or ethnic traditions usually occur at the funeral home or at the cemetery, but are not part of the Mass of Christian Burial or The Liturgy of the Word.

In the Roman Catholic Church there is no designated grieving period. There is a custom to pray for the dead. One day a year is designated for this by a special solemnity in the liturgical calendar: The Solemnity of All Souls, on November 2nd. Local parishes often celebrate this day with special prayers or Mass for those who have died within the past year, inviting families to participate.

Cremation and Times When the Body Cannot be Present in Church

Cremation is permitted by the Roman Catholic Church. Often the body is brought to Church for the Mass of Christian Burial and then taken for cremation.

If cremation takes place before the Mass of Christian Burial, or if the body is not able to be brought to church for some reason, a memorial Mass may take place. At this time, all of the parts mentioned above that apply specifically to the body of the deceased (the clothing of the casket with the pall, etc...) are omitted.

TEACHER EXPLAINS CEMETERY PROCEEDINGS TO STUDENTS

From early childhood, we come to think of the cemetery as a "scary" place. As educators, we need to help children re-think their viewpoint. A cemetery provides the final resting place for the body of the deceased, and a point of focus for the survivors. A cemetery is a place where life can be remembered and honored by placement of a memorial, ie: monument, marker, plaque, or inscription. Cemeteries are designed to provide a pleasant environment for visitation by the survivors.

Before explaining to the students what they will encounter at the cemetery, please have one teacher, representing the school, contact the funeral director in each situation to ascertain the particulars. For example, the body may be lowered into the ground at the conclusion of the committal service, placed in a mausoleum, or remain in a chapel for burial at a later time. The vocabulary and number of details you share with your students depends on the age level you are teaching. Do not rely solely on the following basic explanation.

Funeral Procession

Inform your students that the final step in the ritual of burying a person is to take the body from the funeral home or church service to the cemetery, mausoleum, or crematory. If it is daylight, out of respect for the deceased, the mourners usually drive in a procession with their car lights on and a small funeral flag on the fender of each car. Often a police escort guides the cortege through traffic, and other vehicles are stopped as they pass through intersections.

In geographic areas where the site of the funeral service is in close proximity to the cemetery the mourners may travel the distance on foot. Groups of musicians may accompany the cortege to the grave site.

Committal or Grave Side Service

Remind your students that, during the grave side service, prayers may be offered, Scripture read, or a eulogy given. Family members and friends may speak, read poetry, or recite a work they have authored as their way of saying goodbye. At the conclusion of the committal service, family and friends may choose to leave and return to their homes, or choose to remain and witness the interment.

Interment or Burial

Warn your students when interment is to occur in the presence of the people gathered. Please have accurate information from the attending funeral director as to how this is accomplished in your geographic area. When explaining the workings of the funeral, mausoleum, crematory, church, chapel or cemetery, you need to supply information so the students might better understand what they may see, smell, or hear.

mausoleum:	a building or wall where the casket is placed in its own sealed crypt.
grave:	an open site in the ground prepared to receive the casket. Procedures may vary in the manner the casket is lowered into the opening. Leather straps may be used, equipment with a hand crank may be employed, or a small piece of machinery may be necessary to lower the casket.
columbarium:	a type of mausoleum for cremated remains, with niches in a wall to retain urns.
urn garden:	section of a cemetery designated for the burial of urns containing cremated remains.
scattering:	where legally permitted, cremated remains are strewn at a specific site designated by the deceased or decided upon by the survivors.

If your students ask specifics concerning embalming, cremation, or burial, please contact your area funeral director for comprehensive information.

VII

MEMORIAL SERVICES IN SCHOOL

The memorial or remembrance service is an acknowledgment of loss, a sharing of memories, and a way to make closure and put the absence of that person who died into perspective. Now that is a lot to ask of a twenty to forty minute service. Perhaps a more realistic description would be that this type of service provides the opportunity "to glimpse the possibility of healing."

As concerned as we are about the potential problems that can present themselves when death touches a school community, we are equally convinced about the need for healing actions to take place. When loss through death occurs, our own vulnerability to death is raised to a conscious level. Anxiety clouds our ability to correctly label our emotional reactions. Providing the opportunity for children, adolescents, and adults to "bring their suffering to speech" begins the process of survival. Amid the feelings of fear, confusion, rage, and profound sadness lies the courage and the real need to get on with life.

Healing the pain of grief is a little like healing a deep puncture wound. One can't just ignore the wound or cover it with a bandage and hope for the best. Even at the risk of pain, the wound needs to be cleaned out, medicated, and given the opportunity to heal from its deepest part, one layer at a time. Scars are inevitable, and often unavoidable. Scars should be seen as a sign of healing and survival, not simply an indication of suffering endured.

Establishing an open, trusting relationship with your grieving students will provide them a safe foundation from which to work through their grief.

Providing students the opportunity for a spontaneous non-religious or religious experience can be comforting. This may be a brief service in the classroom, on the campus lawn, or at another significant place. The planning and execution of a memorial or remembrance service provides an excellent opportunity for introspection and an acting out of the "loss" experience. Active and passive participants benefit in a real way.

The school should take the opportunity to set aside a time and/or provide a gathering place for those students, teachers, and staff who wish to attend a formal commemorative assembly. This gathering place could be in the school building, on the school grounds, at a public park, or in the church of the deceased student. This does not preclude students attending the service planned by the family.

The assembly can take place the week of the death or weeks later. Adequate time is needed to prepare this assembly. The faculty advisor chosen to coordinate this effort should be cautious when selecting those students who will create and actively participate in this planned school assembly. While it is natural to choose class leaders who are reliable, organized, and who read and speak comfortably in front of their peers, the faculty advisor should do some investigative work in order to be able to discern which students have a genuine need to be involved. In discussions with students months after the death of a friend, the complaint heard most often is, "The teachers planned it all; then they chose guys to do stuff who didn't even know him when he was alive. They didn't ask his real friends."

When planned with dignity, respect, and attention to the needs of all concerned, such a service leaves people feeling better, a little more in control of their emotions, and encouraged to work through the grief that is now part of their lives.

SERVICE EXAMPLES
Spontaneous and Planned - Religious and Non-Religious

In the following scenarios of the deaths of ten-year-old *Sebastian Greer*, and sixteen-year-old *Anne Singleton* (see IV), we are presenting an ideal response on the part of both teachers and students so that you might include our suggestions if they would be feasible in your particular setting. It may be necessary, due to the size of your school and/or predictable poor behavior of some members of your student body, to plan the memorial in the evening so only those students who might realize the benefits of such a gathering would return on their own time to attend.

SECTION A - PRIMARY OR MIDDLE SCHOOL
Sebastian Greer, ten-year-old fifth grader, private school, accidental drowning:

SPONTANEOUS RELIGIOUS CLASS PRAYER SERVICE:

There were two fifth grade classes at St. Zita's. The teachers met with their classes individually in the morning to read the statement of facts surrounding Sebastian's death, to facilitate discussion, and field questions or comments from the children. Teachers dispensed with regular class work. They played taped music and encouraged the class to make cards for Sebastian's family.

Mr. Corwin and Mrs. Bohl, teachers, read the book, *Hope for the Flowers*, written by Trina Paulus, to their students, and talked about its meaning. During the discussion about this book, many issues surfaced. For example, some of the students confessed that they used to fight with Sebastian on the playground, because he always insisted on being the right forward when they played soccer. Teachers assured the children that their reaction to Sebastian had probably been warranted. The teacher acknowledged how angry the students must have been with him. Mr. Corwin also assured the students that it is not wrong to remember Sebastian's abrasive characteristics while we are remembering his positive qualities.

The school's assigned psychologist, their director of religious education, and the bereavement specialist were on call for any student who needed individual attention.

A sister of one of the students had been a paramedic on the scene of Sebastian's accident. After lunch, she stopped in to speak with the fifth grade classes, which had been gathered together in one classroom. She honestly answered questions. She refrained from lecturing them about "safe play guidelines."

After she left, the teachers asked their students if they would like to put together a prayer service. All were in agreement. In the midst of choosing music, a scripture reading, and setting up, each student wrote a favorite memory of Sebastian.

They did not move Sebastian's desk, but moved all the other desks to face his. The students stood around the room, sat at the desks, or wherever they felt comfortable. On his desk, they placed a thick, brightly colored candle, and a vase, holding the flowers sent by caring friends.

Opening Song:	*Sing A New Song*, Glory & Praise, North American Liturgy Resources. (Chosen because of its familiarity to the children, and could be sung without songbooks. One student said that Sebastian "…never liked draggy songs," and another said that the words made him feel better.)
Lighting of Sebastian's candle:	Gregory Stewart (Sebastian's locker partner and friend) lit the candle as the second verse was sung.

Opening Prayer:	Sara Morris, friend: "Dear God, We are sad that Sebastian has died. We are having a hard time believing it is true. Please take him to Heaven to live with you. Amen."
Reading:	JOHN 11:35 (This and the surrounding Scripture speaks of how hard it was for Jesus when his friend, Lazarus, died.)
Speaker:	Leland, friend. "This is really hard. All I want to say is that we chose this scripture because it makes a lot of us feel like Jesus really understands how hard it is when a friend dies. Mr. Corwin says it's important to do whatever you have to do and say whatever you have to say, and that it only makes things harder to keep your feelings inside. I think it's important to remember everything about Sebastian, so anybody who wants to can come up and put what they wrote in this special basket. If you want to, you can read it out loud."
Sharing of Memories:	Taped instrumental of *Friends,* by Michael W. Smith. Brian walked up to the front of the room, turned around, and very quickly read from his paper: "Me and Sebastian were buddies, right, and once when his dog, Trouble, died, we took it down near the tree house to bury it. Sebastian cried, and so did I. An' that was nothing like what this feels like." (Signed: Sebastian's friend, Brian J. Peters) Leroy stood up and read his note from his desk. Then he walked up and put his note in the basket: "Sebastian wasn't the fastest runner in our class. I could always beat him. But he never got mad or anything. He'd just laugh and say 'I'll get you next time, dirt bag!'" (Signed: Sebastian's buddy, Leroy) Kevin was a good friend of Sebastian's. As difficult as it was, he struggled through the reading of his memory: "Sebastian told me one time that he wanted his tree house to be even bigger and better than the one he plays in when he goes down to his Grandpa's farm. You know, the one that used to be his Dad's. He liked working on his tree house better than anything… said he used to pretend his dad was a kid his age and they were working on it together." (Signed: Sebastian was the greatest! Kevin)

Cheryl was one of the last to bring her note forward. She put it in the basket, then retrieved it, and awkwardly read:

"Last Fall, the chain came off my bike right in front of Sebastian's house. A bunch of the guys were at his house, and they were all making fun and teasing me. I was so mad! I had the hardest time getting my bike home with my books and everything! Later that day, he crossed through the back yards and fixed it. He said he was sorry. I guess it's hard for boys to be nice to girls." (Signed: I'm glad we made up. Cheryl)

Most of the other students simply put their memories in the basket they had set on Sebastian's chair. On the basket had been taped a message:

"You have placed your special memories of Sebastian in this basket. Is that memory now gone? No, it remains with you forever. Our memories of Sebastian will keep him with us always."

Closing Song: *On Eagles Wings*, Glory & Praise, North American Liturgy Resources.

Encouraging Sebastian's classmates to speak their anxiety, their fear and confusion, made their feelings more manageable. Most of these youngsters came away from this service with a more calming perspective, a hint of "I'm going to be okay." There is usually a notable bonding in a class of students who share a mutual experience of this intensity.

PLANNED RELIGIOUS ALL SCHOOL PRAYER SERVICE:

Miss Leisring, Mrs. Ryan, and Mr. Besse, fourth grade teachers, offered to plan the prayer service to be held in church. Since they had taught Sebastian and the rest of the class the year before, their involvement was significant. Their assistance also relieved the fifth grade teachers of an added responsibility.

Students in grades four through eight gathered in church about an hour before dismissal. The prayer service was planned to last from twenty to thirty minutes. Primary grades one through three were excused. Any special requests from younger children to attend because they were in car pool with, neighbor of, etc., were honored, if a written note was sent by parent/guardian. Parents of students were welcome.

Gathering Song: *Eye Has Not Seen*, Marty Hogan, GIA Pub.
(Three of Sebastian's closest friends carried the flowers from his desk, the lighted candle, and the memory basket. They placed these on a table in the sanctuary.)

Opening Prayer:	Rev. Robert C. Calmenetti

"Heavenly Father, we gather before you deeply saddened by Sebastian's death. We come to you seeking comfort. We come to you for understanding. We come to you seeking acceptance. Be present to our needs as we bring you our pain and sorrow. We pray in the name of your son, our Lord Jesus Christ, who suffered, died and rose so that all might have new life with you forever. Amen"

Speaker:	Rev. Calmenetti

"It is good for us to be together to share the pain in our hearts. Being together is comforting. We are all helpless in the face of tragedy. We find peace in knowing that Sebastian is with the Lord. But we need to say aloud that we would rather have him with us. We can't always have our way.

"Each one of you is an important part of this community. Sebastian was important to our school and parish community, too. Not all of you may have known him, but those who knew him well could tell wonderful stories about him. As these next days and months go by it would be good if you could share some of those stories.

"As we pray together this afternoon, I would ask you to be especially mindful of Sebastain's family. They need our love and support, and our prayers. I ask you to be especially mindful of his friends, who are feeling a deep sense of loss right now. Remember Sebastian's teachers and his coaches. And please, pray for me as I prepare for Thursday when we will celebrate the Mass of Christian Burial for this precious child of God - Sebastian Greer."

Song:	*In This Very Room*, sung by the seventh/eighth grade choir.
Speaker:	Mr. Barry Mertin, Director of Religious Education.

"On the table before you, you can see some of the reminders we have of Sebastian's life: flowers, symbolizing the joy and laughter this youngster brought to us; and the memory basket, filled with memories the fifth grade gathered yesterday. You are welcome to add your own memories to this basket; the memories gathered will be given to Sebastian's mother and father later today. The candle's light reminds us that whoever Sebastian may have been to any one of us will live forever in us all.

"The Easter candle symbolizes God's promise of resurrection to all who believe in Him. When you come to the funeral Mass tomorrow, you will notice this candle in a very prominent place, assuring us all of the Lord's presence and his promise to be with us in the midst of our sorrow.

"None of us really understands death - not parents, not priests, not teachers. Most of you have heard the story of Stripe and Yellow in the book, *Hope for the Flowers*. After hearing this story, maybe you were able to think about death without feeling so frightened."

READING: *Hope For The Flowers*, Page 75, Paulist Press, New York, N.Y., read by Lamont Ward, the eighth grade student who tutored Sebastian in Math.

Speaker: Mr. Mertin continues:

"This reading reinforces our belief that life is changed, not ended. Our faith teaches us that, when the accident happened, Sebastian went home to a loving God. Although we will never see, play ball with, teach, tease, or ride bikes with Sebastian Greer again, we know and we believe that he lives forever in the Father's house."

Prayer: Rev. Calmenetti:

"OUR GOD PROMISES AN ETERNAL DWELLING TO ALL WHO DIE BELIEVING IN HIM. HIS FAITHFULNESS TO EACH OF US ENCOURAGES US TO PRAY:"

Mrs. Geldon, Principal:

"We come to you with faith, Lord. Receive Sebastian into your eternal care, we pray to the Lord...."

ALL RESPOND: "Lord hear our prayer."

"We come to you with our sorrow, Lord. See our pain, our confusion, our doubts and our fears. Help us to help each other, and fill us with your love, we pray to the Lord..."

ALL RESPOND: "Lord hear our prayer."

"We come to you with our compassion, Lord. Help us to see the ways we can be your hands and heart to Sebastian's Mom and Dad, as they learn to live in a world without their son, we pray to the Lord..."

Rev. Calmenetti:

"GENTLE FATHER, WE ENTRUST OUR YOUNG BROTHER, SEBASTIAN, TO YOU. WALK WITH US ON OUR JOURNEY TO HEALING. BE OUR STRENGTH AND OUR HOPE. FILL US WITH YOUR PROMISE OF LIFE ETERNAL UNTIL THAT DAY WHEN WE ARE ALL UNITED WITH YOU FOREVER. AMEN"

Closing Song: *When Nature Has Nestled*, Text: Delores Dufner, OFB; Tune: *Foundation*, traditional American Hymn Melody, Acc. Russell Woollen, 1980, Copyright, 1980, ICEL.

SECTION B - HIGH SCHOOL

Anne Singleton, sixteen-year-old junior, public high school, killed by a drunk driver:

SPONTANEOUS NON-RELIGIOUS MEMORIAL SERVICE:

Anne's friends gathered in Room 404 with the permission and encouragement of teachers. The students cried their tears, shared their disbelief, and pieced together facts they had been given. Sometimes the room was very quiet, sometimes they voiced their anger at the injustice regarding the way Anne died. Polly needed to talk about their day of sailing, how much fun they'd had, how they were looking forward to getting together with the boys they'd met on the lake. Patricia needed to talk about all the "what ifs" and "if only's". "If only she had waited till we'd showered, and all gone into town together later." "What if we had all been hit by that jerk?" "If only we'd been with her, we could have warned her."

Their fears and anxiety about whether she suffered a great deal of pain were calmed when Mr. Richards (the principal) sat with them and explained the fact that doctors at the hospital had assured Mr. and Mrs. Singleton that Anne was not feeling pain during her last hour of life at the hospital.

Anne's friends ate lunch in small groups on the campus grounds. After lunch, they gathered on the lawn. Mrs. Leander, the juniors' American Writers teacher, and Mr. Melscher, the school counselor, joined the group. With encouragement, the students began to label their feelings.

Mr. Melscher assured the students, "Whatever you are feeling is okay. Probably the friend sitting next to you right now has the same questions you do. Mrs. Leander and I will try to help you find some answers. Keeping your feelings inside is not healthy. You need to get them out. Hey, Teresa, could you play that tape you were playing at lunch?"

Song:	Teresa played her taped recording of Bette Midler's *You Are the Wind Beneath My Wings*.
	The students gathered their thoughts in the silence that followed. Some awkwardly pulled clover from the grass and knotted the stems together.
Sharing:	DeLyle began: "I feel like Anne is here. With us all thinking about her, I can almost feel her presence. It's weird! It feels good, but it also hurts real bad." Alesia said: "I feel lost. Anne is a good friend. We talk a lot.....we used to talk a lot. I feel so lost." Caleb spoke: "I feel... scared. It could happen to any of us. Anne was so terrific - she didn't deserve this!"

Cheston added:

"Well, I'm mad! Nobody should drink and drive. Anne would be here if it weren't for that damn drunk!"

Lamont said:

"Anne was the best! She made everyone feel important. She never put anyone down."

Paul agreed:

"Anne was the happiest person I ever knew. I'll miss her laugh - her sense of humor. That girl could find the funny side in any situation!"

LaQuita quietly added:

"Anne always braided my hair...she talked me into getting contacts...she helped me pick out my prom dress...I can't believe she's really gone."

Polly could not speak.

Lakeisha said:

"I feel like this is a bad dream or some terrible joke. How are we gonna get the crowd back the way it was?"

Patricia said softly:

"I wish I had made her wait for me. I feel so guilty..."

Janet added:

"I'm glad we're all together. I feel so lonely inside."

Sandi said:

"I feel so bad for her Mom and Dad. I want to go and be with them, but I'm afraid I'll just make things worse."

Dominique agreed with Sandi, and then said:

"A lot of the class didn't even know Anne. I want everyone to know what a special person she was. We can't just bury her and forget!"

Song: Everyone was quiet for a minute or two. Mary Beth pulled her guitar into her lap and started strumming softly and singing *That's What Friends Are For.* When her voice broke, others joined in and helped her finish the song.

The string of clover had become a giant wreath, connecting hearts and hands in friendship, shared pain, and love.

Adult sharing: After a couple of minutes, Mr. Melscher spoke:

"I can hear how deeply you all cared about Anne. And I think, in a very special way, Anne *is* here with us, through your special memories of her and what she means to your lives. You will survive...one day at a time...because you have each other to share the pain we all feel."

Mrs. Leander added:

> "I agree. Your memories of Anne will be your strength. And you are right, Dominique; the whole student body needs the opportunity to remember how special Anne was. We are planning an all-school memorial service on Wednesday, at 1:30 P.M. Any of you who would like to help plan this program are welcome to meet in my room tomorrow during the lunch mod. Just get a hall pass from the office. Before you go back to your rooms for dismissal, you are welcome to look at and borrow some of the media I have gathered for possible use. Feel free to write something yourself, find an excerpt from a book, some poetry, tapes, whatever you feel might be appropriate. We'll pull it all together tomorrow."

The students quietly stood up, and casually returned to the school building.

It is important to note here that the students owned this brief and intimate acknowledgment of their loss. The spontaneous memorial can be effective in any school setting. All that is needed is the willingness of key adults to allow it to happen. It can be a gratifying experience for the teacher to be invited into the young people's lives in such a way.

Teachers, counselors, the school psychologist, and the bereavement specialist were available and used throughout the day as students needed special assistance. A basic, safe frame was established around the day and, within that frame, students who were close to Anne had the freedom to be together, express their feelings, and begin to make closure.

Many of Anne's friends went together to the Singleton's home after school, and were warmly welcomed by Mr. and Mrs. Singleton. They sat out on the back porch and shared stories about Anne with her Mom and Dad. The young people invited them to come to the memorial service at school, and Mr. Singleton thanked them and said they would think about it. The students left with the feeling that they had done a good thing, and that they would be welcomed back anytime.

PLANNED NON-RELIGIOUS ALL SCHOOL MEMORIAL SERVICE:

Mrs. Leander, the American Writers teacher who had an established trusting relationship with Anne's friends, had been asked by the principal, Adam Richards, to coordinate the planning of a memorial service designed to meet the needs of staff, teachers, and students. Anne's friends took considerable time in choosing music and readings which spoke to their needs as well as the needs expressed by others within the school community.

Participants chosen to read or speak were Anne's school/social friends, since her immediate friends decided individually they would have a difficult time speaking publicly.

This memorial was held in the school auditorium where important all-school gatherings were routinely held. This service was in addition to whatever personal arrangements had been made by Anne's family.

Flowers that had been sent to school by friends and neighboring schools were placed in the main hall, the school office, the music room, and in Anne's homeroom.

Troy O'Neill, a fellow student, had been given permission to decorate the stage. He borrowed potted geraniums from the local greenhouse where he was employed on weekends.

A *collage of pictures* of Anne (gathered by friends and affixed to a bulletin board) was placed in the glass-enclosed display case in the main hall entry area. Anne's junior yearbook picture was enlarged at the local fast photo shop owned by one of the junior's parents, and displayed on an easel on the stage. Anne's friends felt that in a large high school it was quite possible that many fellow students might need to be reminded of who Anne was.

A *banner*, painted by students in Anne's Wednesday morning art class, hung on the stage.

Students filed into the auditorium as they normally would for any all school gathering. The mood was quiet, subdued, respectful.

The program proceeded as follows:

Song:	*Bridge Over Troubled Water,* from Simon and Garfunkel's Greatest Hits (tape)
Invocation:	Mr. Melscher, School Counselor (at students' request): "OUT OF UNREALITY, LEAD US INTO REALITY. OUT OF DARKNESS, LEAD US INTO LIGHT. FROM DEATH, LEAD US INTO IMMORTALITY." (Author: Upanishad)
Speaker:	Mr. Richards, Principal: "It is good for us to be together this afternoon. I have felt a real sense of caring as I talked with many of you these past two days. Some of you knew Anne, some of you did not. Some of you were very close friends with Anne, while some were not at all close. The important thing is that all of us realize that a member of our student body has died. Anne's death has touched each of us in a very personal way. We are a wounded community, united in our need to grieve her death and find the courage to move ahead in our lives."

(The principal then reminded students of dates, times and instructions regarding permission slips for those attending the visitation and funeral service.)

Mr. Richards continued:

"...On behalf of the junior class, thank you for all the generous donations collected this morning in homeroom. We are happy to report that you have almost enough to buy that portable keyboard for the music room. On it will be a dedication plaque in honor of Anne. We will make the dedication at an all-school assembly later this year.

"Anne's parents asked me to convey to you their deep appreciation for your concern and support. They especially appreciate the students who have stopped by for a visit with them. They have heard treasured stories about Anne, which they would have no way of knowing if these young people had not been willing to share them. Mr. and Mrs. Singleton have asked me to extend to you an open invitation to stop by any time. As tragic as it is that their daughter has died, they would never want to think they had lost contact with their daughter's friends.

"At this time, the Music Ensemble will present for you their tribute to Anne (a two-year member of this group) by singing a song they performed at the National Chorus Competition last May. When I spoke with some of these students a few minutes ago, they were remembering how excited Anne was that they had received a #1 Rating for all their hard work."

Song: *Candle On The Water,* Al Kasha and Joel Hirschhorn, from the Walt Disney Motion Picture *Pete's Dragon,* The Disney Choral Series. Sung by the Music Ensemble.

Speaker: Dominique LeCroix, friend:

"If you were lucky enough to know Anne, you know that she was one of the most enthusiastic people in this class! She was always ready to organize a party, work on a team, or encourage someone else to 'go for it'.

"When we put the invitation on the bulletin board for people to write down their favorite memories of Anne, the basket in the office was filled by the end of the day. All these notes you put into the memory basket will be given to Anne's family. We want them to know we will never forget how special Anne was to us.

"The Class of 1990 will not forget Anne Singleton. We will remember the way she lived, and touched our lives. We will remember the way she died. Anne was an innocent victim of a man driving under the influence of alcohol. Over the summer, we will be forming a task force, with Mr. Singleton's help, to look into ways we can discourage people from drinking and driving.

"As hard as it is, we must accept the fact that Anne has died. I would like to share something with you that is helping me to get through the day. It was written by Schopenhauer:
'I BELIEVE THAT WHEN DEATH CLOSES OUR EYES WE SHALL AWAKEN TO A LIGHT, OF WHICH OUR SUNLIGHT IS BUT THE SHADOW.'"

Song: *There's Me*, from Music & Songs From Starlight Express (Tape).

Speaker: Kramer Hardesty, friend:

"We are all hurting...and missing Anne already. Each of us is trying to handle her death in his/her own way.

"Some of the juniors arranged those flowers on the stage behind me. I did recognize that the plants were geraniums, but Troy O'Neill had to explain to me that the oakleaf geranium symbolizes friendship, and the silverleaf ones symbolize remembering. They tell us to recall-to remember Anne. Earlier today as I stood watching Troy and the others arrange the plants, I realized I was trying not to remember because it hurt too much. Those intense flowers said, 'Go ahead and remember.'

"Personally, I first met Anne her freshman year when we were both sent to the office for cutting a class. Yeah, she flashed that smile of hers, and gave a dumb excuse, but she still served five days detention.

"You can't help but notice the banner made by the art class for her memorial this afternoon...
'THE SMILE THAT YOU SEND OUT RETURNS TO YOU'

"I don't know about you, but it is hard for me to picture Anne without a smile, unless her team was losing, she had flunked an Algebra II quiz, or she had dropped all her sheet music in the hall for the fiftieth time. I'm not suggesting that any of us can be really happy in the months ahead...or that we should pretend we are over Anne's death. But I am suggesting that you save a smile or a kind word for those other students who were close to Anne. Some of them will want to talk, while some will just want to know you are there. Let's be patient with each other. Let's listen to each other.

"Remember the song we just heard from the Starlight Express, where we heard that no one else can cry the tears we have to cry...but we can share each others' pain. We can be there' for each other.

"Anne loved her friends. She loved her school, and we couldn't think of a more fitting way to say goodbye to Anne than to sing our *Alma Mater*..."

Closing Song: *School Alma Mater*

This type of service can be as creative as the people you gather to do the planning. It is good if, in the beginning, there is an honest expression of feelings, whatever they might be, and then music, readings, poetry, etc., should all progress, at least in theory, towards healing and survival for those gathered.

The time for gathering resources, by the way, is before a death occurs. This is a good project for English and Journalism majors.

A memorial service can be held immediately after the death or weeks later. The form of the service can be structured, religious in nature, or a simple emotional and/or physical journey to a memorable place.

For example, if the student was a member of the school's track team, the other runners and friends may gather at the gymnasium, and begin to walk one of the routes regularly used by the track team. Particular spots would be designated as stopping points so they might be able to share some verbalized memories or prayers.

Ownership, for the most part, should belong to the young people. Needs of the teachers and staff can and should be met in additional ways.

Assisting your students in choosing a way to memorialize a deceased member of your school community through a non-religious or religious program, will allow the young people to make closure and begin the healing process.

LONG TERM MEMORIALS

When feasible, a long term memorial can be considered. A plaque appropriately placed, a tree planted on the school campus, even a page in the year book can satisfy the students need to memorialize a peer who has died.

More elaborate considerations may include any permanent fixture of special meaning or value to the school community.

It is important that students take the initiative in raising the funds, deciding on the purchase, and planning the dedication.

MEDIA SUGGESTIONS

When providing materials for the students to plan a school memorial, you may wish to have available:

BOOKS

Provide books addressing the topic of death (see Chapter IX, RESOURCES). A passage or a page from a particular book might be included in the service.

When the students have decided on a theme for the service, they may find a poem or a quotation to use as a focal point. The parts of the memorial should have a common thread. Collections of quotations, scripture, collected poems, Chinese proverbs, Japanese haiku could be the source for a selection. One excellent resource for a theme is *With Each Remembrance, A Selection of Writings on Memories*, by Flavia Weedn, Roserich Designs, Ltd., Carpinteria, CA.

If the students had decided the focus of the service would be friendship, the following quotation might be chosen: *"A real friend is one who helps us to think our noblest thoughts, put forth our best efforts, and to be our best selves."* (author unknown)

If the student died after a terminal illness, or suffered some disability or hardship, the following quotation might be chosen: *"If you can't have the best of everything, make the best of everything you have."*

Provide a Bible, or a book of Scripture, accompanied by a list of readings that may apply to a death situation. Following is a sample of readings which have been used at other memorials:

Hebrews 13: 1,2	*Speaks of brotherly love and being kind to strangers.*
Isaiah 43: 1-3a	*Assures us that no matter how greatly we are troubled, God will stay with us and we will survive the pain.*
Isaiah 12: 2	*Tells us we need not be afraid for God is with us.*
Ecclesiastes 3: 1,2,4,6	*We are told there is a time for everything - even a time to grieve and cry.*
Psalm 23:	*Consoles us with the thought that even when all is darkness in our lives, the light of healing is possible.*
2 Tim. 4:6-8	*Speaks of faith in an eternal joy that awaits those who trust in God.*
Wisdom 5: 15-16	*We hear that God will reward, shelter and protect the just forever.*
Micah 6:8	*We are told that man's goodness is enough.*
Sirach 44: 8-15	*Agrees that the person who died was so important to us that his/her wisdom will live on forever.*
Isaiah 57: 18-19	*Reminds us that the Creator promises to hear, lead and comfort mourners.*
Romans 8:14	*Assures us God welcomes all who follow Him.*
Psalm 121	*We are assured that the Lord is our protector now and forever.*
Psalm 62	*We hear that God's love is constant.*
Psalm 131	*We are assured that humble trust in the Lord brings us peace.*

MUSIC

Have available tapes and/or records, or a list of music that could be appropriate. Classical music and gospel music offer possibilities which would be acceptable. Religious hymnals contain music that might be comforting. Some popular selections would also be acceptable.

The following list of songs used at other memorial services offers a sampling of possibilities:

"That's What Friends Are For," Dionne Warwick, Stevie Wonder.

"Wind Beneath My Wings," Bette Midler (also a version by Lou Rawls.)

"Bridge Over Troubled Water," Paul Simon, Charing Cross Music.

"Candle On the Water," The Disney Choral Series.

"There's Me," MUSIC & SONGS from Starlight Express.

"Whenever I Call You Friend," Kenny Loggins' Nightwatch album.

"You've Got a Friend," Carole King's Tapestry album, or Anne Murray Favorites.

"Welcome Home," Carole King.

"So Far Away," Carole King.

"Home Again," Carole King.

"Way Over Yonder," Carol King.

"Sometimes," Henry Mancini, Music, Felice Mancini, Words, Northridge Music Co.

"Up Where We Belong," Music: Buffy Sainte Marie and Jack Nitzche; Words: Will Jennings.

"Somewhere Out There," An American Tale.

"Papa Can You Hear Me," Barbra Streisand.

"Forever," Kenny Loggins' Vox Humana tape.

"Rough Side of the Mountain," Album.

"Friends," Michael and Deborah Smith, Meadowgreen Music Co.

"I Have a Dream," Abba.

"You'll Never Walk Alone," from "Carousel".

"Since You Asked," Judy Collins, Rocky Mountain National Park Music Co.

"Try to Remember," from "The Fantasticks".

"Look to the Rainbow," from "Finian's Rainbow".

"Day by Day," from "Godspell".

"Think of Laura," Christopher Cross.

"The Rose," from the motion picture.

"Children Will Listen," from "Into The Woods" (suitable for teacher in-service).

"Lean on Me," Thelma Huston and the Winans, Album/Lean On Me, by Warner Bros.

"In This Very Room," Ron Harris Music.

"Baptism Prayer," Tim Schoenbachler, North American Liturgy Resources, (adapted).

"I Will Be with You," James E. Moore, Jr., G.I.A. Pub., Inc.

"My Soul is Still," David Haas, To Be Your Bread, G.I.A. Pub., Inc.

"Psalm 23," (The Lord Is My Shepherd).

"*Psalm 62,*" (Only In God), John Michael Talbot, Come To The Quiet, Cherry Lane Music Pub. Co.

"*Sing The Song of Life,*" Spirit of Love, Daughters of St. Paul, Boston, MA 02130.

"*Your Song of Love,*" Robert Fabing S.J., N. Amer. Liturgy Resources.

"*By My Side,*" Jay Hamburger, Peggy Gordon, Godspell, The Times Publishing Co.

"*Day Is Done,*" Text: James Quinn, Cassell Ltd., London; Tune: Copyright Oxford Univ. Press, The English Hymnal.

"*Amazing Grace,*" John Newton, Tune: Early American Melody, arr. by Edwin Othello Excell, 1851-1921.

"*Love Is Come Again,*" Text: J.M.C. Crum, 1872-1958, Tune: Copyright Oxford Univ. Press, from the Oxford Book of Carols, Martin Shaw 1875-1958.

"*When Nature Has Nestled,*" Text: Delores Dufner, OFB, Tune:

"*Foundation,*" traditional Amer. Hymn Melody, Acc. Russell Woollen, 1980, copyright, 1980, ICEL.

"*Shepherd Me O God,*" Marty Hogan, GIA Pub., Inc.

"*Arise, My Soul, Arise,*" Betty Ann Ramseth, from Keep In Mind, Augsburg Pub. House.

"*I Am the Bread of Life,*" Suzanne Toolan S.M.

"*You Gave Me Love,*" Medley, Amy Grant, In Concert II (Tape).

"*How Great Thou Art,*" Copyright Manna Music, Inc.

"*I Believe,*" Words and Music, Ervin Drake, Irvin Graham, Jimmy Shirl, Al Stillman.

"*On the Willows,*" Stephen Schwartz, Godspell, Times Pub. Co.

"*Shepherd of My Heart,*" Sandy Patty.

"*Father's Eyes,*" Amy Grant, (Tape of same name).

"*Eye Has Not Seen,*" Marty Hogan, GIA Pub., Inc.

"*Healer of Our Every Ill,*" Marty Hogan.

"*We Walk by Faith,*" Marty Hogan.

"*For Everything There Is a Time,*" Donald J. Reagan, Glory & Praise, NALR.

"*Lord Teach Us to Pray,*" Joe Wise.

"*In the Garden,*" The Rodeheaver Co.

"*Just a Closer Walk with Thee,*" Words: Oscar Clute, 1904. Tune Trentham, Robert Jackson, 1888, Baptist Hymnal, Convention Press, Nashville, TN.

"*Softly and Tenderly,*" Will L. Thompson, 1880, Convention Press, Nashville, TN.

"*He Hideth My Soul,*" Convention Press.

"*Thy Word,*" Amy Grant, Straight Ahead (Tape).

"*Treasure,*" Gary Chapman. (Amy Grant Video)

"*Love Will Find a Way*", Amy Grant, Unguarded (Tape).

AUDIO/VISUAL

Audio visual tapes can be borrowed from your school district's central office, funeral directors, or purchased for an individual school's use.

Below is just a sampling of what is available:

But He Was Only Seventeen, The Death of a Friend, Using the example of a seventeen-year-old killed in an auto accident, this program helps students constructively work through their feelings about death, specifically the sudden death of a peer.

Did Jenny Have To Die?, Preventing Teen Suicide, Students view the details of suicide through the eyes of family members, friends, teachers - and of the victim herself.

Teens Who Choose Life: The Suicidal Crisis, Helps viewers understand the events and feelings that may precipitate a suicidal crisis.

Talking About Death with Children, Explains to the child what death means, why it happens, what happens to the body, and why we have a funeral.

Understanding Grief: Kids Helping Kids, Dr. Earl Grollman developed the helpful advice presented by the narrator, including normal grief reactions and what we can do to help. This program is beneficial for adolescents working through their own grief or helping a bereaved friend.

"Images of Music" Series, "Before It's Too Late," "You're Only a Memory Away," and "Walk In The World For Me." Each song in this series is ideal to use as an introduction or conclusion to a program.

The above audio/visuals can be ordered from BATESVILLE MANAGEMENT SERVICES, P.O. Drawer 90, Batesville, Indiana 47006

The description of the following suggested tape is reprinted with permission of the National Funeral Directors Association:

Share the Secret, Save a Friend, Teens talk openly about their suicide attempts; professionals clear up the myths and examine the causes. The impact of this film lasts because what kids see and hear comes from other kids.

Now with the new NFDA Videotape Rental Program, for a nominal fee your school may be able to rent videotape programs available through the Learning Resource Center. For further information, contact your local funeral director, or the NATIONAL FUNERAL DIRECTORS ASSOCIATION, 11121 West Oklahoma Avenue, Milwaukee, Wisconsin 53227, Telephone (414) 541-2500.

These suggestions are offered merely to stimulate the teacher's creativity in offering options to students. Depending on the situation, there is an endless amount of material available.

VIII

PROCESSING GRIEF

LIFE TRAUMA MAY INTERRUPT THE GRIEF CYCLE

The grieving student may verbally or behaviorally indicate an inability to cope with the recent death. As the teacher, you may find yourself listening to hints of previous unresolved loss issues; for example: divorce, terminal illness, emotional, physical and/or sexual abuse, drug and/or alcohol abuse.

Educators are legally required to report abuse to the appropriate local agency. If the student is under eighteen years of age, the date of the abuse is inconsequential and the incidence must be reported. Only with professional help can the young person work through the devastation of abuse. This loss issue must be addressed first. Grief associated with the death will follow.

In a situation where drug and/or alcohol abuse is present, this abuse becomes the paramount issue. The student will need to associate with a local program or care unit that assists in rehabilitation, before successfully tackling the griefwork.

When a student is part of a family experiencing divorce or a chronic terminal illness, he may need to confront these issues before grieving a death. Be aware of recognized local support groups that speak to the hardships of living with the terminally ill, or being a child of divorce.

In any of the above mentioned situations, academic deficiencies of the grieving student will need to be temporarily shelved, and professional intervention sought. The young person's future mental health is more important than his completing a prescribed school curriculum for a given grade level.

We encourage you to network with other teachers in your city or region, and share information as to which professionals and support groups are serving your community as described in their resource brochure. Use the local grapevine to discover which social agencies follow through. After the referral is made, ascertain if the professional engaged for the student has completed the prescribed diagnostic work up.

71

YELLOW FLAGS INDICATE NORMAL GRIEF REACTIONS

Yellow flags indicate behaviors that suggest caution and attention. The behavior of the student is grief related. The grieving student is gently included in the on-going daily routine.

Your natural instinct may be NOT to enter the world of the grieving student. There is no option on your part; s/he already lives in your school world.

The grieving student returns to your classroom with multiple needs. These needs include a safe, structured environment, patient and empathetic listeners, and enough freedom to do his/her griefwork. Each grieving young person will set personal parameters.

The intensity of the grief reaction will be based on the student's personality type, circumstances of death, and his/her perception of the relationship with the deceased. We cannot anticipate how grief will present itself in an individual student, but we can quell your concerns by listing normal grief reactions.

It is normal for a student to experience great emotional pain.

The grief process has no time limits. Each grieving student's experience will be unique.

Introspection is an important part of healing.

The grieving student may appear pensive and quiet as s/he undertakes subjective speculation.

The student may question "Am I studying and working toward a degree just to end up dead? There is no promise that I will live to accomplish my goals. Why does death take the young, the beautiful and the good? This isn't fair!" The student is meeting his/her own mortality head on. This is expected — this is normal for the initial phase of grief.

Student may have difficulty eating or sleeping.

Sleeping and eating are two issues where quantity is not important, but quality is. The body is responding in a physical way to the pain of grief. If the student is taking in the basic requirement of liquids during the school day, and is able to stay awake during classes, it is evident s/he is not endangering his/her health.

The student may have outbursts of anger.

The grieving student will experience a longing for the person who died. S/he may be embarrassed by a need to regress to a more primitive way of coping. S/he feels helpless and the overt anger is a way of controlling this feeling of helplessness.

The student may over-react to a poor grade, not being chosen for a special assignment, missing the bus, or to someone sitting in "his" or "her" seat. The student may use any opportunity or situation to demonstrate the anxiety s/he is feeling.

It is normal to observe most adolescents wading through conflict. The adolescent is torn between retreating to the security of childhood and entering the world of the adult.

The student may question his/her emotional stability.

A grieving student may sincerely believe s/he is going crazy. The emotions and feelings being experienced are foreign to him/her. The younger child may have no previous experience on which to draw. The child may not yet have the vocabulary to express him/herself. This is a problem you can define.

The student needs information and resources. Supply the student or parent with books or movies that explain or explore grieving. Give them names and phone numbers of respected local support groups for grieving children or young adults, where they can see their feelings are similar to those of other grieving students the same age. (Chapter IX, RESOURCES)

The student may verbalize that s/he sees or hears the deceased.

All grieving persons, regardless of age, have a need to make closure. The grieving student will seek out ways to complete unfinished business. The grieving young person may need to ask questions or itemize his/her own plans for the future. S/he will talk to the deceased and s/he *will* hear the answers and advice. The grieving student may see the presence of the dead parent, friend, or sibling when s/he most needs a sign. This is normal unless this phenomenon becomes a chronic condition interfering with reality.

The student may experience wide mood swings.

Grieving students do not choose to be sad, depressed, confused, or inattentive. The smallest reminder of their loss may set them off, and they will need to leave the classroom. It is easier for the young person and the teacher if the grieving student has been given permission to go to a pre-arranged location in the school building when s/he has the need. Mourning is necessary, hard work and, at times, those rememberings hurt.

Some days the student has energy and appears to be "him/herself". An anxiety filled issue may have been resolved. For example: the grieving student may have made the decision about whether to apply to a university in the next state, or relinquish that dream, and attend the local college in order to stay at home with the newly-widowed parent. Each resolved issue encourages the student to address another area of concern. The younger child pays more attention to his/her instincts. At a particular level of stress or sadness, the younger child gives himself/herself permission to be distracted, to forget for a period of time. At home, when grief is overwhelming, the child may simply go outside and play.

Encourage your grieving student to take some time out for play, for fun, to recharge emotional batteries. At the same time, encourage the student to find a safe haven, a special friend with whom s/he can sort out all the good and bad memories.

Student expresses anger at being forced into a new role.

The student experiences anger at being...fatherless or motherless...at being the only child now... or being the oldest child now...or having no sister at all now... or at no longer being a twin. S/he has been thrust into a new role. Through no fault of his/her own, the student's familiar self-identity has been drastically altered. The grieving student may mistakenly feel s/he must replace or fill the shoes of the dead parent or sibling. The young person needs time to grow into the new role, and to 'get successful experiences under his/her belt'. The student needs affirmation that the unique person s/he is remains undamaged.

The teacher has a unique role to play as a trained observer of the grieving student's behavior. How active you are with a grieving student depends on the previous relationship established with this person. If there were restraints, tensions, or simply a conflict of personalities, your professionalism will warrant that you feed your observations to a different resource. If the student is more comfortable with the school librarian, the chemistry teacher, or the school nurse, please give the grieving student permission to go to that person when his/her grief becomes oppressive.

Please make sure the student has made contact with a trusted adult who will continue to walk with that grieving young person for as long as needed. Because a major amount of the student's life is school centered, it is necessary that staff, faculty and peers be aware of how they can be supportive during this long healing process.

RED FLAGS INDICATE ABNORMAL GRIEF REACTIONS

When we speak of a grief process, we always describe mobility, a flow, an attempt to adjust to the change. When we view abnormal grief reactions, the person has turned away from grieving and has substituted an activity which allows him/her to deny his/her pain. The guidance counselor for each school will need the individual teacher's input and observations as s/he works with the grieving student.

Occasionally, the young person may not respond to the care and support offered by the guidance counselor and the teachers. In this rare situation, outside professional assistance in working through grief is a positive step in the journey toward healing. The teacher should be able to recognize when a particular grieving student needs help.

Professional intervention is indicated:

If the grieving student displays protracted periods of hyperactive behavior, and is unable to stay focused on school work for any length of time, professional intervention is indicated.

If the grieving student avoids speaking of the death to you or any other teacher and has no known resource outside the school with whom s/he shares his/her feelings, professional intervention is indicated.

If after a complete physical examination by a trusted personal physician the student continues to manifest physical symptoms like those of the deceased, professional intervention is indicated.

If the grieving student has cut him/herself off from all old relationships that could provide understanding, empathy and compassion, professional intervention is indicated.

If the grieving student has drastically changed relationship style - even if some adults perceive this change as positive - for example, the grieving student becomes acutely responsible, or ultra patriotic, or intensely religious, professional intervention is indicated.

If the grieving student, however justified, is displaying unbridled, continuous hostility, professional intervention is indicated.

If the grieving student is continuously apathetic and spiritless on all levels of communication, professional intervention is indicated.

If the grieving student is using drugs and/or alcohol to cope with stress, professional intervention is indicated.

In consideration of the amount of structured, quality time spent with the young person, the teacher is in an excellent position to discern what is acceptable and exceptionable behavior for the grieving student. The intense emotion and prolonged time given to a specific behavior is what labels the aforementioned activities as abnormal grief reactions. These behaviors are red flags and warrant outside professional help.

COMMUNICATING THROUGH ART

For a variety of reasons, the student may be unable to verbalize his pain, his frustrations, his fears, confusion and needs. It is then that we use other means at our disposal to help us recognize the trauma within a grieving student.

No young person is indifferent to the experience of the death of a family member. In one way or another, this student will speak his needs. Expression of feelings through art is a safe medium in which to cry, to shout, to express anger, to show fear, to exhibit frustration, or to show loneliness. Often, the simple acknowledgment of those feelings expressed through art, by the teacher, will be all they need to get through the day.

In some situations, Art Therapy may be indicated.

ART THERAPY
Michele Monahan Sanzere, Art Therapist, Children's Psychiatric Hospital of Northern Kentucky:

In addition to observing changes in behavior, you, the teacher, may note differences in the child or adolescent's work, including their art work. This may entail the work itself or the process, for example *how* they go about doing their work. You may need to ask yourself, "Does s/he have difficulty concentrating or investing in their work when no problem was evident before? …Does their work appear significantly different? … or, Do you find yourself feeling uncomfortable when you look at the work due to certain factors or images presented?"

As an Art Therapist. I am often asked what the meaning is of specific symbols and images. Though some symbols can be said to have universal meanings, they may also have a very personal meaning for the creator of the art work. Therefore, it would be unfair to over-interpret or immediately judge a student's work by saying "this means that", or by becoming alarmed and jumping to conclusions without first exploring this further with the student. Meanings can be more easily established by talking with the student and by observing continuing patterns in his or her art work.

Studies of the art work of bereaved children and adolescents in Raymer and McIntyre's book, *"The Art of Grief,"* indicate symbols commonly found in their art work. In brief, these symbols include monsters, rainbows, balloons, birds, roads, time, dead trees, fire, lightning, a large face lacking body parts, and a lack of hands and feet in the figure. Again, Raymer and McIntyre stress the importance of discussing the student's work with him/her before any possible projection of meaning can be made.

While a student may try to avoid speaking of death and his/her own feelings of grief, and though s/he may try to minimize others' concerns by seeming apathetic or trying to display a facade of being "fine", it is likely that the child or adolescent will be less able to censor his/her own art work.

In my own work in Art Therapy, I have encountered numerous students who verbally attempt to deny their feelings or lack any acknowledgement of these, which often include the feelings of loss and grief. Visually, however, their work often suggests otherwise.
One teenage boy who experienced repeated losses, became withdrawn and aloof when apparently overwhelmed with feelings he was unable to express verbally. This was observed

not only in what he drew, but also in how he drew and the process he went through. For example, some days he could barely make a mark on the paper while on others he would fill the entire page with scribbled lines. Each of these observations could be noted as significant and reflective of his struggle to work through a myriad of feelings from loneliness to intense chaos due to the disruption in his life that was related to the losses.

Another case involving a young girl was interesting due to her tendency to work very well on such given tasks as a drawing or painting, yet upon completion, she seemed to need to draw or paint heavy lines over her work, usually in a dark color.

In such cases as mentioned, or with your students who indicate the need for professional intervention, Art Therapy may be a resourceful option.

Some additional advantages of Art Therapy include, but are not limited to, its ability to give a sense of control when the individual may be feeling powerless and helpless in his/her loss. Through the use and mastery of the media the child may regain a feeling of control.

Art materials are the therapists' tools; therefore, the media are not chosen at random but rather for specific reasons depending on what it is that the therapist is trying to elicit or provide. For example, different materials are easier to control than others due to their inherent structure. It is very different working with a medium such as paint rather than a pencil. Though paint may allow more freedom in its fluid make-up, it can also be very frustrating if an individual is not comfortable with its looser qualities. Therefore, the art therapist needs to be familiar with a wide spectrum of media choices, and the advantages and limitations of each one, so that materials are selected appropriately, according to the needs of the client.

Another benefit of Art Therapy is in its ability to facilitate appropriate expression of thoughts and feelings. The tasks and media directed by the therapist can help to channel the energy from the individual's fears, frustrations, and questions into something productive whether it is a drawing, painting, sculpture, etc.

A third advantage is its potential to offer reflections and objective distance from feelings in order to gain insight. By putting his/her ideas down on paper, the individual is provided with some perspective of the experience.

Art Therapy also offers the ability to allow an individual to express and communicate his/her thoughts, even when words do not seem to be available or just do not seem like enough. Children sometimes lack the vocabulary to articulate accurately, and often find it more natural to work on issues through visual images. To have artistic ability is not a prerequisite for the Art Therapy client so it is therefore not limited to those who seem artistically gifted.

A fifth advantage is in its ability to offer non-threatening, success oriented experiences to build or repair a self-esteem possibly shaken by the loss experience. Art Therapy also tries to create a safe environment in which the individual is provided a means to practice problem solving and coping skills.

Lastly, Art Therapy provides a permanent visual record of the client's work. The client can review his/her work at any time and visually note any movement or lack of it s/he has made in working through his/her grief.

Art Therapy can be a valuable and instrumental method of working in the field of child and adolescent bereavement.

IX

RESOURCES

NATIONWIDE SUPPORT AND INFORMATION
THE AMERICAN ART THERAPY ASSOCIATION, INC. (708) 949-6064
1202 E. Allanson Road
Mundelein,Illinois 60060
AMERICAN ASSOCIATION OF SUICIDOLOGY (A.A.S.) (303) 692-0985
2459 South Ash
Denver, Colorado 80222
(AUTOEROTIC ASPHYXIA) (602) 945-0342
A.E.A. National Headquarters
The Bereaved Parents, Inc.
P.O. Box 3147
Scottsdale, Arizona 85251
THE CANDLELIGHTERS 1-800-366-CCCF
CHILDHOOD CANCER FOUNDATION (202) 659-5136
1901 Pennsylvania Ave. N.W.
Suite 1001
Washington, DC 20006
CHILDREN'S HOSPITAL (Local)
Pastoral Care Department
COMMUNITY MENTAL HEALTH SERVICES or
COMMUNITY INFORMATION & REFERRAL SERVICES
Refer to local telephone listing

THE COMPASSIONATE FRIENDS (708) 990-0010
P.O. Box 3696
Oak Brook, Illinois 60522
(for parents who have experienced the death of a child)
DOUGY CENTER, THE
P.O. Box 66461
Portland, Oregon 97266
(center for grieving children)
FERNSIDE: A CENTER FOR GRIEVING CHILDREN
P.O. Box 8944
Cincinnati, Ohio 45208
NATIONAL HOSPICE ORGANIZATION 1-800-658-8898
1901 North Moore Street (703) 243-5900
Suite 901
Arlington, VA 22209
PARENTS OF MURDERED CHILDREN (513) 721-5683
100 East Eighth Street, Suite B41
Cincinnati, Ohio 45202
SUPPORT GROUPS FOR GRIEVING CHILDREN
Listed in local area telephone book under
UNITED WAY. Ask for the Information and
Referral Help Line
SURVIVORS OF HOMICIDE VICTIMS (513) 721-5683
100 East Eighth Street, Suite B41
Cincinnati, Ohio 45202
SURVIVORS OF SUICIDE (S.O.S.) (303) 692-0985
2459 South Ash
Denver, Colorado 80222
UNITED WAY INFORMATION AND
REFERRAL HELP LINE
Provides phone numbers of local support
groups and agencies for information
about a specific illness.

BOOK LIST FOR STUDENTS

There is a vast number of books which can be used to assist children in understanding that their questions and fears regarding death are not unique. We have reviewed six of many books available so that you might have an idea of how they could fit into your lesson plans.

IT MUST HURT A LOT, Doris Sanford and Graci Evans, Multnomah Press, Portland, Oregon 97266, 1986.

Joshua experiences anger, blame, and sadness after his pet dog is accidentally killed. Joshua shares special secrets with the reader, i.e. "My friends want to help, they just don't know how." At the conclusion of this warmly illustrated book, Joshua calls on his personal experience with loss to help a friend whose grandparent has just died. On the inside cover are ten suggestions for an adult concerned about talking with a grieving child.

THE FALL OF FREDDIE THE LEAF, Leo Buscaglia, Ph.D., Charles B. Slack, Inc., Publisher; Holt, Rinehart and Winston, Distributors.

A simple, provocative, story of life and separation for anyone who has suffered a permanent loss. Using the analogy of nature this twenty-seven-page (words & photographs) book speaks of the delicate balance of life and death to adults and children. Each page is a gentle invitation to speak about death.

HOW IT FEELS WHEN A PARENT DIES, Jill Krementz, Alfred A. Knopf, Inc., Publisher.

Photographs of, and interviews with, eighteen children, ages seven to sixteen, who vividly describe their experience of a parent's death. Included are their responses to the positive and negative things people did following the death.

CHILDREN ARE NOT PAPER DOLLS...a visit with bereaved siblings, Erin Linn, The Publisher's Mark, Incline Village, NV 89450.

Before the return of the grieving sibling to the classroom, classmates need to be made aware that their reactions are important. The sections on school and friends will give the teacher a vehicle for introducing the issue.

LOSING SOMEONE YOU LOVE, When a Brother or Sister Dies, Elizabeth Richter, G.P. Putnam's Sons, New York, 1986.

Photographs of, and interviews with, sixteen young adults, ages ten to twenty-four, who describe the death of a sibling, to disease, accident, and murder. The students openly share their regrets, fears, wishes, and sorrow.

TEEN SUICIDE, Janet Kolehmainen and Sandra Handwerk, Lerner Publications Company, Minneapolis, MN, 1986.

Presents six situations where teens are involved in, and affected by, a contemplated, and/or attempted, and/or completed, suicide of a teenaged friend. The case studies deal with warning signs, intervention, guilt, and grief.

Fernside: A Center For Grieving Children compiled the following book list for children who have experienced a death. Your school may wish to have these books available in your school library for teachers and students:

TITLE/AUTHOR	READER AGES	SUBJECT
A RING OF ENDLESS LIGHT L'Engle, Madeleine	13-18	DEATH OF GRANDPARENT
A TASTE OF BLACKBERRIES Smith, Doris Buchanan	6-12	DEATH OF SIBLING
ACCIDENT, THE Carrick, Carol	2-12	GENERAL-DEATH OF PET
AM I STILL A SISTER? Sims, Alicia M.	6-12	DEATH OF SIBLING
ANNIE AND THE OLD ONE Miles, Miska	6-12	AGING
ARKANSAW BEAR, THE Harris, Aurand	7-12	DEATH OF GRANDPARENT (A PLAY)
BEAT THE TURTLE DRUM Green, Constance	6-12	DEATH OF SIBLING
BLACKBERRIES IN THE DARK Jukes, Mavis	6-12	DEATH OF GRANDFATHER
BUTTERFLIES, GRANDPA AND ME Conley, Bruce H.	2-12	DEATH OF GRANDPARENT
CHARLOTTE'S WEB White, E.B.	6-12	GENERAL-GRIEF
CHILDREN ARE NOT PAPER DOLLS Linn, Erin	6-12	DEATH OF SIBLING
CHILDREN FACING GRIEF Romond, Janis Loomis	6-16	SIBLING GRIEF
CHRISTY'S LOVE Johnson, Maud	13-18	TEEN DEATH-INJURY
CHRISTY'S SENIOR YEAR Johnson, Maud	13-18	DEATH OF BOYFRIEND
DEAD BIRD, THE Brown, Margaret W.	2-7	DEATH AND GRIEF

DEATH BE NOT PROUD Gunther, John	13-18	DEATH OF SIBLING
EYES OF THE AMARYLLIS, THE Babbitt, Natalie	13-18	GRIEF
FALL OF FREDDIE THE LEAF Buscaglia, Leo	5-12	DEATH
FIRST SNOW Coutant, Helen	6-12	DEATH EXPLAINED BY GRANDPARENT
GOODBYE CHICKEN LITTLE Byars, Betsy	7-12	DEATH OF UNCLE AND PARENT
GROVER Cleaver, Vera and Bill	6-12	SUICIDE OF PARENT
HEAVEN HAS A FLOOR Roberts, Evelyn	2-7	DEATH OF PARENT
HOPE FOR THE FLOWERS Paulis, Trina	6-18	GENERAL-GRIEF
HOUSE WITHOUT A *CHRISTMAS TREE* Rock, Gail	6-12	DEATH OF MOTHER
HOW IT FEELS WHEN A *PARENT DIES* Krementz, Jill	7-18	DEATH OF PARENT
I HEARD THE OWL CALL *MY NAME* Craven, Margaret	13-18	GENERAL-GRIEF
I'LL MISS YOU MR. HOOPER Stiles, Norman	2-6	DEATH AND GRIEF
IF I SHOULD DIE BEFORE I *WAKE* McDaniel, Lurlene	13-18	DEATH OF SIBLING
ISLAND OF THE BLUE *DOLPHINS* O'Dell, Scott	6-14	GENERAL-FEELINGS
IT MUST HURT A LOT Sanford, Doris	2-8	GENERAL-GRIEF
LAST WEEK MY BROTHER *ANTHONY DIED* Hickman, Martha W.	2-10	DEATH OF SIBLING

LEARNING TO SAY GOODBYE	8-18	DEATH OF PARENT
Leshan, Eda		
LITTLE PRINCE, THE	6-18	GENERAL-GRIEF
DeSaint Exupery, Antoine		
LITTLE WOMEN	12-18	DEATH OF SIBLING
Alcott, Louisa M.		
LOSING SOMEONE YOU LOVE	10-18	DEATH OF SIBLING
Richter, Elizabeth		
LOVE STORY	14-18	DEATH OF YOUNG WIFE
Segal, Erich		
MAGIC MOTH, THE	6-12	DEATH OF SIBLING
Lee, Virginia		
MASK	13-18	DEATH AND GRIEF
Minihan, John		
MY GRANDPA DIED TODAY	2-6	DEATH OF GRANDPARENT
Fassler, Joan		
MY GRANDSON, LEW	2-8	DEATH OF GRANDPARENT
Zolotow, Charlotte		
MY TWIN SISTER ERIKA	6-14	SIBLING DEATH-TWIN
Vogel, Ilse M.		
NANA UPSTAIRS, NANA DOWNSTAIRS	2-8	AGING-DEATH
DePaola, Tomie		
NO TIME FOR GOODBYES	16-18	TRAGIC DEATH-GRIEF
Lord, J. Harris		
SADAKO & THE THOUSAND PAPER CRANES	7-14	SIBLING (LEUKEMIA)
Coerr, Eleanor		
SADDEST TIME, THE	8-12	DEATH-YOUNG UNCLE (ILLNESS) SCHOOL BOY (ACCIDENT)
Simon, Norma		
SECRET GARDEN, THE	12-16	DEATH (PARENTS, AUNT)
Burnett, Frances, H.		
SOMETIMES IT'S OK TO BE ANGRY	6-12	GENERAL GRIEF
Colant, Mitch & Crane, Bob		
SOUNDER	6-14	GENERAL GRIEF
Armstrong, William H.		

X

TERMINAL ILLNESS

The patient who has a terminal illness is not the only victim. The trauma of the terminally ill person becomes the trauma of his/her entire family. This chapter will address the needs of your students when a parent is dying, when a sibling is dying, and when a student in your classroom is dying.

Although the teacher cannot prevent or change anything this student will experience, s/he needs to understand what is happening, so that when the student is feeling overwhelmed, the teacher can clarify options, offer alternatives and suggest constructive, safe outlets.

Empathy is an acknowledgment of the student's personal pain and ongoing turmoil. This chapter is included to encourage your understanding of, and patience with, the student whose family is experiencing a terminal illness.

WHAT IS HAPPENING...
...WHEN THE PARENT OF A STUDENT IS DYING

The terminally ill parent is fighting for his/her life. It does not help to judge their actions. The following examples occur repeatedly in the homes of the terminally ill and usually imprint on the student.

1. The terminally ill parent may put unrealistic demands on the sons and daughters. The hurtful behavior may be due to medication, or the parent may be anxious because he/she sees this as a last chance at parenting. The young person may feel frustrated.

2. The parent may take out frustrations (at a seizure or limitation of movement) by yelling at the children. The young person can build up resentment and transfer this anger to the classroom.

3. The terminally ill parent may demand so much time of the well parent, the caregiver, that the young person loses the attention of both parents.

4. If the well parent needs to spend many hours at the hospital, the young people may be left to run the house and prepare the meals.

5. The terminally ill will focus on self and have little interest in the accomplishments of the young person, and no interest or energy to talk of the future. The student may read this as rejection.

6. Close to the time of death, the dying parent will begin to withdraw and the young person may view this as desertion or abandonment.

7. Children often view sickness and accident as a punishment for some action they performed, or as the consequence of a wish they made.

THE TEACHER WILL REALIZE THAT THE TERMINALLY ILL PARENT HAS LOST THE MAJORITY OF CONTROL OVER HIS/HER LIFE, AND IS ATTEMPTING TO BRING MEANING TO HIS EXISTENCE. IN RESPONSE, THE STUDENT MAY BE STRUGGLING WITH FRUSTRATION, RESENTMENT, REJECTION, ABANDONMENT AND/OR GUILT, AND THE STUDENT BRINGS THESE FEELINGS INTO THE CLASSROOM. FAMILY CARE SUPPORT GROUPS OR A LICENSED MENTAL HEALTH PROFESSIONAL CAN GUIDE THE FAMILY IN CREATING A HEALTHIER ATMOSPHERE IN THE HOME.

...when the young person observes the care giver parent.

The student with a terminally ill parent is observing not only the decline of the parent who is dying but the emotional ravages on the healthy parent.

The parent in the role of care giver is under immeasurable strain. On any basic one-hundred-point stress chart for anxiety related situations, the care giver parent will easily amass one hundred stress points without having to read the complete list. There can be little doubt that they are hanging on to what we term a "normal existence", by their fingernails.

1. The well parent may feel the need to do it all alone, until s/he is physically exhausted and his/her health is threatened.

2. The care giver may have a "Superman Complex", always on the alert, always checking the amount of medicine left for the next dosage, always having the gas tank filled and clothes laid out for an emergency trip to the hospital in the middle of the night. One wife described herself as Wonder Woman, "... but someone took away my golden lasso!"

3. The healthy parent may be fearful as s/he watches a spouse use the stairs, run machinery, or mow the lawn. S/he may not feel able to leave the patient for fear that something will happen while s/he is gone. The student may never have any family representation at sporting events or school functions.

4. The young person may be aware of the financial worries of the well parent.

5. The student may overhear relatives or neighbors criticize the care giver parent when s/he leaves the house for some needed rest and relaxation.

6. The young person may hear zealots tell the care giver that if s/he prays well enough, hard enough, long enough, his/her spouse can be saved.

7. The student may see himself as sole emotional support to the well parent. Friends and relatives may socially isolate the family out of fear of contagion, fear of what they might happen to see, or because of a misplaced idea that the family needs privacy. Often, the extended family (i.e. grandparents, aunts, uncles…) are in such distress they extricate themselves from the family. The young person loses the support of the extended family when it is most needed.

8. The young person may see and imitate the parents "life as usual" attitude, while inside the fears go unanswered. When the child and teenager are shielded from the truth, they can only imagine a death more painful and disfiguring than what the patient will experience.

THE TEACHER REALIZES THAT THE STUDENT IS TORN BETWEEN WANTING TO SUPPORT THE HEALTHY PARENT AND WANTING TO RUN FROM WHAT S/HE SEES HAPPENING TO THE HEALTHY PARENT. THE TEACHER CAN ENCOURAGE THE STUDENT TO SHARE HIS/HER FEARS, WORRIES OR CONCERNS WITH THE WELL PARENT. THE WELL PARENT SHOULD BE ENCOURAGED TO ANSWER THE CONCERNS OF THE STUDENT AND/OR SEEK HELP FROM A MENTAL HEALTH PROFESSIONAL.

…when the student looks toward the future.

"Mom, if you need to get out of here and get a job, or go back to school, I won't judge you. I could stay at home with Dad. You need a life, too. I know you love Dad, maybe you are just not in love now."

Mother was in the hospital again. The son and his father went out for dinner and returned to an empty house after dark, when the child asked, "This is how it's going to be, isn't it, Dad? Will we be able to do it without Mom?"

"The kids at school say Dad looks funny since his operation. They are scared of him, and won't come to our house anymore."

"The worst part will be going back to school without a mom."

"Can we stay here, or will we have to move?"

"Dad, will your friends still be your friends after Mom dies?"

"If I don't have a life now, what will it be like after Mom dies?"

"Can you work, Mom? Will you be good at it?" The mother playfully replied, "Well, I keep looking in the want ad's, but so far, nobody seems to need a thirty-two-year-old majorette."

THE TEACHER REALIZES THAT STUDENTS WORRY ABOUT THE FUTURE DURING THE TIME WHEN A PARENT IS DYING. THE STUDENT NEEDS PERMISSION TO VOICE PERSONAL CONCERNS TO AN OBJECTIVE LISTENER, WITHOUT FEAR OF BEING MADE TO FEEL GUILTY, SELF-CENTERED, OR INSENSITIVE. THE TEACHER KNOWS THAT MOST CONCERNS WILL BE RESOLVED AS THE STUDENT WORKS THROUGH HIS/HER GRIEF FOLLOWING THE DEATH.

WHAT IS HAPPENING...
...WHEN THE SIBLING OF A STUDENT IS DYING

The dynamics present in the home where a sibling is dying may include continual turmoil.

1. The sibling may have to adopt an adult role in the home that includes more responsibility. This young person may have to assume the housework, the cooking, and mothering the younger children, as the parents care for their dying child. The student then returns to the classroom and is expected to fit in with his/her peers.

2. Siblings in the home of a terminally ill young person may come in for their share of conscience pangs because of their behavior toward their dying brother or sister.

3. Siblings may well feel a certain amount of jealousy or anger because the parents spend so much time with the sick brother or sister.

4. If the terminal patient is at home, the siblings may have to help with the nursing duties. The brother or sister may be repulsed at having to feed, change or bathe the patient.

5. The parents may show a leniency with their sick child that they do not show the others. Their well children will most often find this "unfair"!

6. Young people will not usually verbalize their displeasure over the turmoil the sick brother or sister has brought into the home, but they may display their hurt toward someone else. For example, s/he may be involved in repeated fights on the school bus.

7. The sibling may assume s/he is the next to become ill and die because they share the same environmental and genetic background.

THE TEACHER REALIZES THAT SIBLINGS MAY VIEW THEIR HOUSE AS A PLACE OF TENSION AND SADNESS, RATHER THAN A SANCTUARY CALLED HOME. THE TEACHER CAN HELP ORGANIZE SUPPORTIVE FRIENDS OF THE FAMILY WHO CAN ASSIST IN THE DUTIES OF CARING FOR THE TERMINALLY ILL SIBLING, OR PROVIDE SOME HELP IN MEETING THE COMMITMENTS ASSOCIATED WITH THE WELL SIBLINGS.

FOR SUPPORT FROM OUTSIDE THE SCHOOL COMMUNITY, ADVISE THE PARENTS TO CONTACT UNITED WAY (SEE RESOURCES-IX) FOR HELP AND/OR ADVICE FROM A SPECIFIC AGENCY AND/OR SUPPORT GROUP.

The following examples will illustrate how one high school responded to Claudine, a sophomore whose brother, Blake, was dying from a rare form of cancer. When a student's sibling is dying, it takes the efforts of many people like the art teacher, the volleyball coach, and the math teacher (in examples below) to keep the student in the main stream.

1. The biology teacher included in his lecture on blood cells, a description of the ravages of cancer. He did not forewarn Claudine or ask if she needed to be excused that period. Claudine later complained that the teacher could have requested some input, or apologized for the light manner in which he covered the topic. She was upset not by the subject matter, but by the teachers attitude, "He left out all the pain."

2. The art teacher helped Claudine survive the months of watching her brother die. The teacher gave Claudine a note that read, " My good friend died when I was eighteen. If you want to talk, I can listen."

3. The school activity club called her home and asked if Claudine would volunteer time to baby sit for couples who wished to attend a class on parenting. Claudine declined, adding "Nobody is helping my family; my mother is doing it all alone."

4. Claudine was grateful to pass Algebra II. It was only because her Math teacher arranged for a member of the Junior/Senior Math Club, to stop by a few evenings a week to help her with homework.

5. The high school volleyball coach encouraged the team members to take turns picking up Claudine for practice. He suggested they arrive at her home early enough each evening to run in and say hello to Blake.

WE CAN NOT PREDICT WHAT YOUR STUDENT WILL NEED IN THE WAY OF SUPPORT. YOUR NEIGHBORHOOD AND SCHOOL COMMUNITY IS RICH WITH PEOPLE WHO CAN ACT AS RESOURCES. THE TEACHER CAN HELP DEFINE THE PROBLEMS CONFRONTING THE STUDENT SO OTHERS WILL KNOW WHERE AND WHEN THEY CAN STEP IN AND OFFER SUPPORT.

WHAT IS HAPPENING...
... WHEN A STUDENT IN YOUR SCHOOL IS DYING

This section is not intended to educate you on working with the terminally ill, but it will suggest some practices the school can initiate to help the young person who is dying, the siblings of the young person who is dying, and the school community.

When a student in your school is terminally ill, a good rule of thumb is to notice what fellow students say or do that makes the terminally ill young person more comfortable. Students who are sincerely interested may ask, "Do you always hurt?" "What does that tube do?" " Show me how your wheel chair works." The ill young person may decline to answer or may give a detailed explanation. Most fellow students will respond with empathy, not pity. Follow their lead.

The following examples will illustrate how one school responded when a fourth grade student was dying:

ELYSE FARDON: A FOURTH-GRADER WITH A TERMINAL ILLNESS. SIBLING: ONE BROTHER, PATRICK, SIXTH GRADE

1. It was doubtful that Elyse would ever return to the classroom, but she still considered herself a part of the fourth grade. Pictures of Elyse, sent by the parents, were shared by the teacher with her classmates, so they gradually saw the progression of her illness. Weekly snapshots of her classroom assured Elyse that her friends had not forgotten her.

2. Mr. and Mrs. Fardon gave permission for the school to contact Elyse's physician for a clinical explanation of the illness. It was suggested that a representative from the Education Department at the Children's Medical Center visit the fourth grade to supply the students with an accurate description of Elyse's illness, and field any questions the children might have. (Children of all ages need to be told in so many words that an illness, like nephritis or leukemia or heart disease is not contagious.)

3. A bulletin board was set aside in the classroom for Elyse's work, assuring the other students that she was still a contributing member of their class.

4. A math computer was sent home for her use.

5. The principal made a point of visiting Elyse once a week. The following suggestion was included each Monday in the all school announcements: "If anyone has a card, message, or drawing to send Elyse Fardon, please bring it to the office tomorrow morning. I will be visiting her after school."

6. The sixth grade teacher made contact with the parents of Patrick's school friends. This group of parents volunteered to assist Patrick in getting to after school activities, and offered assistance in completing school science and art projects that always seemed to require adult supervision, library research, or supply gathering.

The following examples will illustrate how one school responded when an eighth grade student was dying:

PHILIP: AN EIGHTH-GRADER WITH A TERMINAL ILLNESS.
SIBLINGS: TWO SISTERS - JANE, FIRST GRADE, AND SYDNEY, SEVENTH GRADE, ATTENDING THE SAME SCHOOL

1. Philip was not always able to attend class but his parents were intent on keeping up his spirits. They involved him with school work, hoping he could graduate with his eighth grade class. (Sick people need power. They need to preserve their identity.) Mr. Fee, Philip's tutor, volunteered to visit each of the classrooms when Philip was absent for any length of time. He explained to the students how Philip would look when he returned to school after a stay in the hospital. He cautioned the fellow students about callous remarks that could hurt Philip. He made sure that everyone understood that the most anxious or frightened students may be the ones who would have a need to act out or make flippant, ridiculing comments.

   The first day back at school went very well. Philip chose not to wear a hat or wig, even though chemotherapy had claimed all his hair. He was nervous about being accepted, but was comfortable after the reception he received from his well-informed fellow students.

2. Philip's sister, Jane, a first-grader, was experiencing reading problems. Realizing the family could not afford the extra time Jane needed for review each evening, her teacher asked if Jane could be placed in the reading van even before the semester grades were due. The strategy was to keep Jane from falling so far behind that she would not be able to pass into second grade at the end of the year.

3. Sydney, Philip's twelve-year-old sister, was being badgered by one teacher about keeping up with her assignments. The parents were constantly having to reassure their daughter that they knew she was trying her best to complete all her work. The parents finally wrote the teacher a note, "This is all the homework Sydney could do tonight. Sydney has never had trouble with grades before this year. We are not the type of parents to interfere, but under the circumstances, please give her some latitude."

4. At another point, Sydney missed a week of school due to illness. When she returned to school, her physician wrote the teachers asking that she be permitted to leave class "… if she appears overwhelmed." His prescription was for "limited stress, and understanding."

   The teachers responded by arranging with the school nurse to provide a safe place for Sydney to use as a retreat until she was able to return to the classroom.

5. As Philip's condition deteriorated, the students were given basic information on a daily basis by the principal or Mr. Fee, who were in contact with the family.

When a student (or teacher colleague) is dying of a terminal illness, it will seem natural to plan ahead for the time when he or she is not there. Some may argue that it will be easier on the students if the transition is quick and smooth and well-thought-out ahead of time. In reality, the students need to own a part of that transition. At the time of death, the awkwardness, the void that exists, gives credence to the significance of the person who died. The students need to be part of the process of acknowledging what is now missing from the classroom. This is good griefwork for everyone, and it opens the door to accepting the painful transition.

THE TEACHER REALIZES THAT WHEN THE TIME SPAN BEFORE THE DEATH IS HANDLED OPENLY AND RESPECTFULLY, THE MOURNING PERIOD FOLLOWING THE DEATH TAKES ON THE SAME DISPOSITION. WHEN THE DEATH DOES OCCUR, THE TEACHER WILL BE DEALING WITH A DEEPLY SADDENED GROUP OF CLASSMATES AND FACULTY, RATHER THAN A FRENETIC, ANXIOUS CROWD OF TEACHERS AND FELLOW STUDENTS.

Conclusion

During a terminal illness, the entire family is continually off balance, constantly adapting because each day is different. Along with the futility of trying to adapt to all the changes is the knowledge that no matter how hard they try, their family cannot return to the way it was. They are helpless. The student brings that feeling of helplessness to the classroom. The school day may be the one consistent component of the student's life during this time of waiting.

The teacher certainly cannot be all things to the student. However, it is important for the teacher to have as much insight as possible as to how this student may present him/ herself in the classroom. This information may not solve the problems encountered, but it will help to define the situation.

The student needs understanding, not pity; the student needs encouragement, not added pressure; the student needs support and clear headed objectivity at a time when his world is very dark. The student needs permission to laugh in the midst of pain, and to hope in the midst of sorrow.

XI

ESPECIALLY FOR THE TEACHER

WHEN A TEACHER IN YOUR SCHOOL DIES

If a teacher in your school is near death…

The anxiety level in a school where a faculty member is terminally ill can be overwhelming. When a teacher is dying, the faculty that has met and supported each other in their anticipatory grief is usually better equipped to be present to their students at the actual time of the death. The faculty and staff should not hesitate to rely on outside bereavement specialists to meet with them as a group and help them discuss personal fears and concerns.

If a teacher in your school dies…

At the time of a teacher's death, adapt the guidelines in Chapter IV, WHEN A STUDENT IN YOUR SCHOOL DIES, and Chapter VII, MEMORIAL SERVICES IN SCHOOL. The faculty may wish to have an additional private memorial for their colleague at a time the students are not present.

If you are hired as an interim or permanent replacement for the teacher who died…

You deserve to have facts made available so that you might better understand your new students and their needs.

The grieving students may unconsciously react to significant dates regarding the death of their teacher (birth date, death date, sports banquet, senior class play, graduation), you need to be apprised of pertinent dates in writing, so you can anticipate and recognize needs. Ignoring these occasions will only heighten the anxiety. Be assured some casual school friends may have completed their grieving, while the close friends will find it more difficult to accept the finality of the death.

You will be involved daily with many hurting people. When a teacher in a school dies, everyone in the building is affected…the students, the faculty, the office personnel and maintenance staff. Establish your own credibility with your new students. Once they can define what they have lost, you will find them more ready to accept necessary changes. A sincere interest in listening to other faculty members and students as they talk about the role "Mr. Hobart" played in the school community will accomplish two things: one, you will provide them an opportunity to talk about their loss, and, two, you will gain valuable insight into changes that may need to be implemented.

Major changes will naturally cause anxiety, so at first you will want to make only those changes absolutely necessary. Even before you make minor changes, such as re-arranging the room to your liking, or changing the bulletin boards, you might comment to the students on how unique the room appears to you. Allow them to explain why furniture has been placed in a certain way, or ask them how to interpret charts displayed on the bulletin board. If you can manage to keep things the same for a period of time, the transition to new operating procedures will be less abrasive.

Give students the opportunity to explain Mr. Hobart's method of grading. Agree that his methodology was workable. Then outline your valid reasons for needing to change the grading procedure. It may take them a little time to get used to your ways.

…the important thing is to recognize that what your students may object to, or complain about, or resist, is probably NOT the real issue. When they emotionally protest a procedural change, they may be, in reality, protesting the death of their teacher.

THE NEEDS OF TEACHERS AND STAFF

Once the immediate reactions of the students have been dealt with, you will observe the varying needs within the school community. The intensity of the grief you observe will naturally depend on the relationship each individual had with the person who died. The principal mourners involved may include staff personnel, the school nurse, the special tutor or music teacher of the child who died, the librarian, school psychologist, principal, maintenance technician, or co-teacher. Each of these person must discern their individual needs. If you are the teacher who guided the grieving students through the immediate time after death, your needs may be quite different from those of another faculty member.

If your unresolved grief over a previous loss is getting in the way of sharing this important time with your students, please consider talking with someone you trust. On a personal level, acknowledge the fact that your emotional needs are valid. A resurgence of feelings regarding any death you may have experienced in the past is common and to be expected. Do not minimize your need to work through any personal feelings that have come to the surface.

If you have experienced the death of a spouse, parent, brother, sister, friend, or some other special person in your life, and although you felt you had come to terms with this loss, you may find there are issues which now need your attention. Before you can listen to the regrets and fears of your students, you will need to come to some closure and acceptance of your own previous grief experiences. If you find yourself still uncomfortable talking about death, you will have difficulty listening to your students. Be up front with your guidance counselor. Invite him/her to be in the classroom with you as your students absorb the news of the death.

No matter how well you responded during this critical time, recognize the fact that a death in the school takes its emotional toll on everyone in a position of leadership.

You must take the time, and find the means, to meet your personal needs and recharge your batteries. Seek the type of follow up care that appeals to your personality, and choose the means that you find comfortable:

1. Investigate educational resource material dealing with grief.
2. Schedule a teacher in-service day that would address teacher's personal death awareness and/or unresolved loss issues.
3. Discover inspirational books that speak to your pain.
4. Talk with a supportive, non-judgmental friend, such as the guidance counselor.
5. Acquire tapes on normal grief reactions.
6. Seek the advice of a clergy person who is trained to work with grief issues.
7. Find time to be alone.
8. Organize a school support group that would meet weekly to discuss unrealistic expectations, and share suggestions on how to minimize pressure.
9. Solicit outside professional grief counseling.

*"WORRY DOES NOT EMPTY TOMORROW OF ITS SORROW,
IT EMPTIES TODAY OF ITS STRENGTH."*
(Author unknown)

XII

LONG TERM SUPPORT OF THE GRIEVING STUDENT

Because no two students will respond to a death in the same manner, we can only speak in generalities.

We cannot tell you to be strict or lenient, but we will ask you to find that fine middle line that is only discovered after careful observation and intent listening.

Adults complain of confusion and memory loss when dealing with death, and so it is with young people. Yes, the student needs to understand the material covered in class, but if s/he is handing in a blank test paper, offer to meet with the student and substitute a verbal quiz. If the student is covering the required school work, waive the busy work for a specified period of time.

We realize that as a teacher you are expected to be accountable for your time in the classroom, but when a group of students is anticipating a death, or experiencing the aftermath of a death, you will need to be flexible. We promise you that you will see the rewards of this flexibility.

A student was killed in a fire. Weeks later, during an English grammar class, the students were diagraming sentences. The third sample sentence read: "The old man saw the blazing fire from the road, and realized he could not summon help quickly enough to save the burning building."

The teacher realized by the hush in the room that most of his students were remembering how their fellow student had died. He closed his grammar textbook, and asked "Does anyone need to talk? I sure do." If the teacher had skipped that sentence, or ignored the hush in the room, he silently would have been telling his students, "I'm too busy to acknowledge your feelings. You are making others uncomfortable."

In the weeks and months that follow a death significant to your students, we are not suggesting that you set aside "grief time", but we are asking you to respond when the need is evident, or the classroom data being presented offers a teachable moment.

LETTERS FROM STUDENTS DESCRIBING TEACHER INTERACTION

We encourage you to read the following letters and profit by the counsel, complaints, and suggestions:

Dear Teacher,

I was thirteen years old, in the eighth grade, when my brother, Joshua, died. He was the youngest in the family and everyone at school knew him. I don't recall what any of the teachers said when my brother died, but I do remember the actions of one teacher; simple as the action was, it showed she was grieving with me. She reached out as I walked by and touched my shoulder. She didn't try to use words to make it all better. Not until years later did I realize how I had needed that small sign of affection and how much that touch (her gesture) meant when I was so painfully missing Joshua.

Dear Teacher,

Our friend, Courtney, was killed in November. The following April, on her birthday, six of us met at the cemetery after school to leave some flowers, tell some stories, sing Happy Birthday, and laugh and cry together. The following day in school I made the mistake of mentioning to you what we had done at the cemetery. You turned on me and told me we should all be ashamed of ourselves for being so ghoulish. You then instructed me to make sure none of the group who had gone to the cemetery mentioned it for fear word would get back to Courtney's parents. Well, Courtney's parents already knew because we had gone from the cemetery that day to their house with flowers for her mom and dad. They hugged us and thanked us for remembering Courtney's birthday. I never did figure out why you were so upset. Did you think Courtney's parents would forget it was her birthday if nobody mentioned it?

Dear Teacher,

After the death of my parents, my grandparents raised me for seven years. Last year, when I was in sixth grade, my grandfather died suddenly. Tuesday, the day after his funeral, I told my grandmother I was returning to school but instead I walked for hours in the park. Wednesday, I did go back to school and was given a detention, to be served all day the following Saturday. Nobody asked me why I skipped.

Dear Teacher,

When my sister, Chantal, died it was helpful to have teachers acknowledge in some way that they knew what had happened. In a large high school, moving from class to class, it was important for each teacher to ease the tension by making an initial gesture. It was difficult when a teacher never mentioned Chantal's death, or acted like it didn't happen. I remember how difficult it was just to go to school. I found it difficult to sit still and concentrate. A few months after Chantal's death, I handed in an essay exam totally blank. I could not concentrate enough to answer even one question; it seemed so utterly pointless. The teacher took me aside and asked what the problem was. She already knew. We talked and she agreed to give me a verbal exam.

Later in the year, some teachers would ask me how I was doing. This was important to me because the first few weeks you receive a lot of attention and support. After that you seem to be on your own. It is lonely. Some teachers seemed impatient and uncomfortable with my grieving. This was a very hard time for me.

Dear Teacher,

I was in the second grade when, over the weekend, my teacher, Mrs. Gamble unexpectedly died. On Monday morning we had a new teacher. I can still see that new teacher sitting at Mrs. Gamble's desk, cleaning out drawers. She was throwing our Friday afternoon art work papers into a big wastebasket. I saw her throw away the paper on which I had made a tree with a sponge dipped in green poster paint. I can still recall the anger of an eight-year-old child at that teacher! The last thing Mrs. Gamble had said to me that Friday afternoon was "Lisa, your tree is very pretty."

Dear Teacher,

I was only in high school two months when my father died. All the teachers from my old grade school came to the funeral home. As sad as I felt, it gave me a good feeling to know they remembered my Dad. They remembered how he attended every school musical, how he helped re-wax the gym floor, and how badly he played volley ball at the annual parent/faculty game. I felt less lonely.

Dear Teacher,

Most of my teachers were too easy on me when my Mom died. It seemed like they would let me do anything I felt like doing. During that time I guess I needed more structure. I had been a very good student but I just didn't care anymore. I think teachers should have personal conferences with the kids of deceased parents to determine how the student feels about being treated as a special student. I was in a crisis situation. It was my special case, my own problem, my own feelings. Each person is different. Listen to the student.

Dear Teacher,

I recall coming home and having to tell my parents that I had failed a "Death and Dying" quiz. I was in the fifth grade and was confused because I thought I understood more about death and dying than anyone else in the class. My sister had been killed four months earlier.

The teacher had explained the answers to the class after our graded papers were returned. One true/false question was: "The final stage of grief is acceptance." I answered "false". To me acceptance meant that it was okay, and death wasn't okay at our house. Another statement was: "It is easier for someone with faith in a religion to accept death." I had answered "false" because I knew our family was hurting and confused in spite of our religion. I tried to explain my answers but the teacher just added insult to injury by telling me that faith makes us stronger than someone with no faith. It was one thing having failed the quiz but I felt I had also failed at being a good Christian.

Dear Teacher,

Our classmate, Bethany, died on the soccer field of an undiagnosed heart problem. The following day in school some prayers were said for Bethany, and that was the last time her name was mentioned in the school building. I remember all of us crying for days. Classes went on as usual, and our tears were ignored.

My mother spoke with the principal, and offered to have Bethany's classmates meet at our home with some of the teachers to talk about the death. My mother was told "Under no circumstances should the students be upset further. Time will heal." We were made to feel that our emotions were not normal reactions to the loss of a friend. What a terrible year!

Dear Teacher,

We were in sixth grade when my twin brother was killed. I overheard the seventh grade teacher tell my teacher "I'm glad you've got the surviving twin in your class, and not me. I simply couldn't talk about it." I can't tell you how much I dreaded going into the seventh grade.

Dear Teacher,

When my mother was diagnosed with a terminal illness, we moved in with my maternal grandmother. My sixth grade teachers were made aware of the situation. At age twelve, I learned very quickly that if people knew your mother was dying they treated you differently. I desperately wanted to be like the other kids, so as time went on I stopped telling people.

My grandmother took care of me, and, as soon as I was old enough, I got part time jobs to help keep food on the table. The day my mother died we did not contact the school. When the school office called our home to verify my absence, Grandmother informed them of my mother's death, and then asked them if I was going to get in trouble for missing two days of classes.

My school counselor, Miss Nepeit, came to Mother's funeral, mentioned that she had spoken to my teachers about my absence, and assured me that she would collect my assignments until I returned. Over the next three years that same counselor invited me to join support groups held for students who had experienced a death. She supplied me with information that helped me make decisions about courses. My senior year in high school she spoke with my grandmother concerning college, assisted me in filling out financial aid forms, and made me aware of grants and scholarships.

Maybe you are saying to yourself, "Well, that was her job." But it was not so much what Miss Nepeit did over the years, but the way she did it. She seemed to know that I valued being independent, and gave me all the space I needed to work through my grief. I felt secure knowing that, even if I didn't want to talk or join a group, she would be there for me when I was ready. She never told me how I should be feeling or that I should be over the death of my mother. She helped me regain some control over my life. For all the grieving children out there, I hope your school has a least one Miss Nepeit.

Dear Teacher,

My father died when I was a fifth grader. Two years later, in my seventh grade English class, we were reading poetry. The subject of the poem centered on the death of a father. I just started crying, right there in class. My teacher appointed a classmate to lead a discussion about the poem, and motioned for me to leave by the back door. He met me in the hall and we walked by the principal's office, where he ask for someone to take over his class.

We walked outside, sat on a wall, and talked about the poem and my dad. He understood I didn't have any control over those tears. I don't recall anything special he said, but I do know that when we finished talking, I was not embarrassed at my show of emotion. He did not in any way insinuate that showing my feelings was a sign of weakness. I felt comfortable enough to go to my next class.

Dear Teacher,

When my only brother died I felt so alone that I just gave up. My grades plummeted and I started getting into trouble at school and at home. I kept telling everyone that I was okay, and to leave me alone. I had slowly constructed an "I don't give a damn!" wall around myself. I was obnoxious. One day, Mr. Cress, my History teacher, physically blocked me in the hall. All he said was "I can see you are hurting. Take this name and number, and give them a call." He handed me a brochure about the Fernside Center for Grieving Children. I stuck the brochure in my notebook and forgot about it. What I couldn't forget was the way Mr. Cress looked at me. He really cared.

A couple of days later, I retrieved the brochure, showed it to my parents, and we eventually did go to the center. Months passed before I could look back and see how Mr. Cress had thrown me a rope when I was at the bottom of a very deep hole.

Dear Teacher,

There were three of us who had always played together, Matt, Carmen and me. When Matt was killed, I had all my other classmates for support, but Carmen attended a private school where nobody had even heard of Matt. I told my teachers about Carmen, and they invited him to attend our school memorial for Matt. I was glad Carmen was there. I needed to be with him as much as he needed to be with us.

Dear Teacher,

My mother died in August just before I began first grade in a new school. My teacher, Mrs. Greene was very attentive, as I recall, through the months of Halloween and Thanksgiving. Everything to me, at age six, was measured in holidays.

At Christmas time, Mrs. Greene instructed the class to make a card for mothers and fathers. I followed her instructions and, to the dismay of my father and sisters, placed the card addressed to "Mom and Dad" under the Christmas tree.

Later that school year we created Mother's Day cards. Again, I followed instructions, and arrived home with my card "To Mother". My sister, Marsha, was furious! She wrote across the card "Should a first grader have to remind his teacher that his Mom is dead?"

The following year in second grade, my teacher, Miss Lao, helped smooth out the rough edges of producing art work for the holidays. At Christmas, she suggested I make a special card for my Dad. For Mother's Day, she invited me to make a card for any special person to let them know how much I appreciated them. I made a card for my two sisters. I can even remember what I printed on that card "You are both like a Mom to me."

Dear Teacher,

I was eleven years old when my nine-year-old sister died. Bonnie lived two years after the automobile accident. She was in the hospital ten months, and an invalid at home until she died in her sleep one night.

In my sophomore year in high school, I started having some serious grief reactions. I just missed Bonnie so much. It seemed like I cried all the time. Everything going on around me seemed so unimportant compared to my pain. Everyone my age had problems, but I had more than my share. All the sadness I had kept locked inside seemed to explode at one time.

I got involved in a support group for grieving teens, but that was not what I needed. I started seeing a grief therapist and that helped. In my junior year, the problems in school worsened. I was always a good student, but my grades went down the tubes because I missed so much school. I'd get dressed for school and pick up my friend, but when we got to school, I just couldn't walk in the door. When I did have the courage to get to the classroom, I would see my sister in the halls and in every empty desk. She would have been a freshman - she never got the chance.

The principal and the teachers were intolerant. They could not comprehend how a death five years previous could be affecting a junior in high school. My parents and the grief therapist met with school officials in an effort to convince them of my needs. They rejected the diagnosis that my problems were grief related and labeled me a school phobic. Maybe if they would have just hung in there with me, I would have graduated with my class instead of dropping out of school.

Dear Teacher,

My mother died the day before my senior year began and it was a shock to the majority of my high school. Only one of my teachers, Ms. Rodriguez, even knew my mom was sick. She had become a friend over the summer when I needed someone to talk to. The morning that school started, I went in and she gave me a hug and said she was sorry. You know, that was really all I needed. As the months went on, she continued to be there even if it was just a smile in the hall. She was never overbearing. She allowed me to be me. This is what I appreciated the most.

Two months after the death, Miss Brendan, my homeroom teacher, confided in me that she also, as a teenager, had experienced the death of her own mother. Her evident survival helped me to believe I would live through this pain and constant sadness. As the months went on, whenever I would get in a real downer, I knew I could turn to her and see a smile, or get a hug, or have someone to talk to - someone who had been where I was and had made it.

Dear Teacher,

I was nine years old and in the third grade when my friend, William, was killed by a hit-and-run driver. All of the parents were notified by telephone within hours after his death. After my parents told me about William, they decided it would be upsetting for me to attend school the following day.

School began at 8:00 A.M. At 9:00 A.M., Mr. Tackett, the principal, was at our home, sitting in our kitchen, explaining to my mother how important he felt it was for me to be at school with all my peers. I was the only one absent. My mother drove me to school and walked me to the classroom. My friends immediately welcomed me. Even as children, they instinctively knew it was good for us to be together.

We spent that first day as a unit. Some classes were held, but if you just couldn't sit still or if you started to cry, it was okay. Nobody made fun of anybody. I remember we asked the adults a lot of questions. We needed all those answers. By the end of the school day, I was still very sad about William, but I wasn't scared anymore. I have always wondered how I would have handled William's death over the years if Mr. Tackett hadn't come to our home that morning.

TEACHER INTERACTION BECOMES AN ONGOING ATTITUDE OF "I'M HERE. I CARE. I CAN TAKE IT. YOU CALL THE SHOTS." STUDENTS NEED TIME TO RE-ESTABLISH SOME CONTROL OVER THEIR OWN LIVES. GRIEVING STUDENTS LOOK TO TEACHERS FOR OPTIONS AND GUIDELINES, NOT DIRECTIVES OR PITY.

Child of mourning...

You should not know this kind of grief. Life is new for you, a beginning that should not be marred by the pain of death.

Yet here you are, wounded and bleeding in my classroom! I can see clearly in your eyes the sadness and fear that overwhelms you.

You look to me for something, and all I want to say is that I am overwhelmed, too. I cannot take away the pain that consumes you, or the terror that panics your sense of well being. I cannot take away the aloneness that separates you from your classmates.

I want to give you back your innocence and your trust in all of us who seek to lead you into the world of adulthood. Yet I know that is impossible. You have been terribly cheated but, somehow, I need to reach beyond the great abyss of your shattered spirit, and touch that part of you that will survive.

You may not know this yet, but you will survive - scarred perhaps, and changed, but somehow stronger for the journey you will have traveled..... if only we can all give you the time and the room you need to work through your grief.

I look into your lost eyes, your sad and angry eyes, and know that I do have the power to make a difference. I cannot make it all better. I cannot erase the truth of your sorrow...but I can see a new child before me this day - wounded, needy, and searching for some glimpse of hope in a world that has let you down.

I will not smother you with my need to console you, but I will let you know I am here for you if you choose to confide in me.

I will not pretend that you can put your grief aside when you walk into my classroom, but I will give you every opportunity to be "just another kid" if that is what you need today.

I will not lose sight of the fact that this is a long journey on which you have embarked, not one of your choosing, but one of necessity if you are to heal the wound of your grief. You are not the only one who will need patience, you know.

I will not let go of you - hold fast to the life line, child of mourning - there are a lot of us out here holding on to you. And if each one of us who cares does our part, you will find your path to healing.

Afterword

Allow your students to see your helplessness.

Together you will grow beyond the awkwardness, the fear, and the sorrow into healing.

Your students may not yet realize the gift you have offered. Please allow us to thank you for them - until the day they can look back and realize how you helped them survive.

BIBLIOGRAPHY

Bowlby, J. Attachment and Loss: Loss, sadness and depression (Vol.III). New York: Basic Books, 1980.

Bowlby, J. Grief and Mourning in Infancy and Early Childhood. In Psychoanalytic Study of the Child (Vol XV). New York: International Universities Press, 1960.

Cassini, Kathleen K. and Rogers, Jacqueline L. I Want To Help But I Don't Know How. Cincinnati, OH: Griefwork of Cincinnati, Inc., 1985.

Czillinger, Kenneth. A Time To Grieve (cassettes). Kansas City, MO: N.C.R. Publishing Co.,1980.

Davidson, Glen W. The Hospice. Washington, New York and London:
Hemisphere Publishing Corporation, 1985, 1978.

Ford, J. Massyngbaerde. The Silver Lining: Scriptural Wake Services. Mystic, CN: Twenty-Third Publications, 1987.

Grollman, E.A. Talking About Death: A Dialogue Between Parent and Child. Boston: Beacon Press, 1970, 1976.

Grollman, E.A. Concerning Death: A Practical Guide for the Living. Boston: Beacon Press, 1974.

Grollman, E.A. Suicide Prevention Intervention Postvention. Boston: Beacon Press, 1971.

Jackson, E. Telling a Child About Death. New York: Hawthorn Books, 1965.

Kastenbaum, Robert J. Death, Society, and Human Experience. St. Louis: The C.V. Mosby Co, 1981.

LeShan, Eda. Learning to Say Goodbye: When a Parent Dies. New York: Macmillan, 1976.

Linn, Erin. Children Are Not Paper Dolls, a visit with bereaved siblings. The Publishers Mark, 1982.

Lucas, Christopher and Seiden, Henry M. Silent Grief, Living In The Wake of Suicide. New York: Charles Scribner's Sons, 1987.

O'Malley, Sarah and Eimer, Robert. In the Potter's Hands: nine wake services. San Jose, CA: Resource Publications, Inc., 1988.

Powell, Marvin. The Psychology of Adolescence. Indianapolis and New York: The Bobbs-Merrill Co., Inc, 1963, 1971.

Rando, Therese A. Grieving: How To Go On Living When Someone You Love Dies. Lexington, Massachusetts and Toronto: Lexington Books,1988.

Rando, Therese A. Grief, Dying, and Death. Champaign, Illinois: Research Press Co,1984.

Rosen, H. Unspoken Grief: Coping with Childhood Sibling Loss.
Lexington, Mass: Lexington Books, 1986.

Schiff, Harriet Sarnoff. The Bereaved Parent. New York: Penguin Books, 1977.

Schiff, Harriet Sarnoff. Living Through Mourning, finding comfort and hope when a loved one has died. New York: Viking-Penguin Inc., 1986.